Design for
Learning

This book is dedicated to children everywhere who are constructing knowledge—especially George Yvon Gagnon and Nina Josephine Collay, our children. They have been our greatest teachers.

Designing
for
Learning

Six
Elements
in
Constructivist
Classrooms

George W. Gagnon Jr.
Michelle Collay

CORWIN PRESS, INC.
A Sage Publications Company
Thousand Oaks, California

For information:

Corwin Press, Inc.
A Sage Publications Company
2455 Teller Road
Thousand Oaks, California 91320
E-mail: order@corwinpress.com

Sage Publications Ltd.
6 Bonhill Street
London EC2A 4PU
United Kingdom

Sage Publications India Pvt. Ltd.
M-32 Market
Greater Kailash I
New Delhi 110 048 India

Printed in the United States of America

Library of Congress Cataloging-in-Publication Data

Gagnon, George W.
    Designing for learning: Six elements in constructivist classrooms /
by George W. Gagnon, Jr. and Michelle Collay.
        p. cm.
    Includes bibliographical references (p.   ) and index.
    ISBN 0-7619-2158-3 (cloth)
    ISBN 0-7619-2159-1 (pbk.)
    1. Constructivism (Education) 2. Learning, Psychology of.
I. Collay, Michelle. II. Title.
LB1590.3 .G34 2000
371.102—dc21   00-011021

This book is printed on acid-free paper.

01   02   03   04   05   06   10   9   8   7   6   5   4   3   2   1

Corwin Editorial Assistant:	Julia Parnell
Production Editor:	Denise Santoyo
Editorial Assistant:	Cindy Bear
Typesetter/Designer:	Marion Warren
Cover Designer:	Michelle Lee

Contents

Foreword

Will you, won't you, will you, won't you, will you join the dance?

—Lewis Carroll, *Alice's Adventures in Wonderland.*

This small, precious book is big and seminal. Small and precious because it modestly, pointedly, and succinctly enhances a slowly escalating revolution in how educators think about teaching and learning. Big and seminal because it contributes hundreds of original strategies to a quarter-century-old educational paradigm shift, a shift from behaviorism-inspired, omniscient teaching to engaged, intrinsically motivated student learning.

George Gagnon, a math teacher, and Michelle Collay, a music teacher, are teachers of teachers as well as seasoned school consultants, but they are much more than that. At home, they are a loving, married couple and the caring, conscientious parents of two preschoolers; they are understandably concerned that their children, Von and Nina, reap the benefits of healthy and effective learning environments when they start school. As professionals with the creative flair of a mathematician and a musician, they are close and interdependent partners; one might say that they are metaphorical choreographers and dancers in the creative design and implementation of teaching *for* learning.

The content of this well-written ballet-of-a-book is not about the staged allocation of M&M candies or the lockstepped use of stopwatches to render timely reinforcement as we might see in the theater of direct instruction, teacher control, and extrinsic student motivation. No, in their musical score, we do not hear the claps, clicks, murmurs, and barely audible yeses of B. F. Skinner's disciples. Nor do Gagnon and Collay ask us to imagine students as what Paulo Freire (1970) cynically called bank deposit vaults storing teacher-delivered knowledge. No, this book tells how to encourage all students to dance together to support one another's deep learning.

This book should be read by neophyte and seasoned teachers, by teacher educators in colleges of education, and by trainees in preservice programs. It should also be read by school administrators for insights into how to improve teacher supervision and staff development, by open-minded behaviorists looking for alternatives to direct instruction, by liberal arts professors who want to learn how to teach so that their students want to keep on learning, and by parents with children in school or with children they are schooling at home. For that matter, everyone concerned with formal education should read this book unless, of course, they already have signed the Faustian pact to search only after the qualities and techniques of authoritarian, direct instruction.

The book's theme is *constructivist learning design* (CLD), which embodies Gagnon and Collay's foundational concepts. *Constructivist* refers specifically to the assumption that humans develop by engaging in the personal and social construction of knowledge. We humans make personal meanings for ourselves and we create shared meanings with others. Thus, humans construct knowledge; we do not receive and internalize predigested concepts without simultaneously reacting to them and engaging them within our own mental maps and previous experiences. *Learning* signifies that the primary goal of schooling is student development and improvement. Teaching should be but one means to that end and as such is secondary in importance to it. Gagnon and Collay point out that it is better to be a guide on the side than a sage on the stage. *Design* denotes the overall structure and outline, sequence of parts, and general forms through which educational activities flow. It is like the composer's or arranger's score for the dance of students and teachers learning together. In other words, Gagnon and Collay's CLD aims to present teachers with a constructivist perspective on how to arrange classroom events for student learning.

CLD is composed of six basic parts flowing back and forth into one another in the actual operation of classroom learning: situation, groupings, bridge, questions, exhibit, and reflections.

1. The *situation* frames the agenda for student engagement by delineating the goals, tasks, and forms of what Gagnon and Collay call the learning episode.

2. *Groupings* are the social structures and group interactions that will bring students together in their involvement with the tasks and forms of the learning episode.

3. *Bridge* refers to the surfacing of students' prior knowledge before introducing them to the new subject matter. The bridge is at the heart of the constructivist methodology; students are better able to refocus their energies on new content when they can place it within their own cognitive maps, values, attitudes, expectations, and motoric skills.

4. Fourth, *questions* aim to instigate, inspire, and integrate students thinking and sharing of information. Questions are prompts or responses that stimulate, extend, or synthesize student thinking and communication during a learning episode.

5. An *exhibit* asks students to present publicly what they have learned; this social setting provides a time and place for students to respond to queries raised by the teacher, by peers, or by visitors about what Gagnon and Collay call the "artifacts of learning."

6. *Reflections* offer students and teachers opportunities to think and speak critically about their personal and collective learning. This encourages all participants to synthesize their learning, to apply learning artifacts to other parts of the curriculum, and to look ahead to future learning episodes.

Although the six features of CLD are vital to its effective implementation, Gagnon and Collay wisely caution us about the absolute necessity of establishing a positive, affective climate as an integral feature of it. A sense of trust, safety, and community in the class and school must be wrapped around and woven through CLD for deep student learning to take place. In classrooms, students and teachers must build a culture of social support and mutual helpfulness complemented by an appreciation of diversity as accompaniments of CLD. Trust between teachers and students and among the students is critical to CLD's success. A collegial sense of support, mutual helpfulness, and an appreciation of diversity also should develop among staff members of a school if classes are to benefit from CLD. Gagnon and Collay help us understand that their creative work on learning circles supports the realization of these conditions.

I invite you now to do as I have done. Read this fine book three times. Read it first for a general understanding of its concepts. Read it again and reflect on your own practice. Read it a third time to engage its ideas as you would engage dance partners. Then keep the book at your side for reference to its many action ideas. Will you, won't you join Michelle and George in their creative dance, so that you will be ready to use CLD in dancing with Nina and Von and other young students in a few years?

—Richard A. Schmuck
Professor Emeritus,
University of Oregon

Preface

Educators undertook several reform efforts during the 1990s. These efforts produced outcome-based education, national and state standards, performance assessments, proposed mandated national tests in reading and writing, national board certification of teachers, and, in many states, revised rules or requirements for graduation. Few educational reform efforts have succeeded, however, in changing the ways schools are organized and students are taught. In *Who Will Save Our Schools?* Linda Lambert and colleagues (1997) contended that real reform in education will take place only because of grassroots efforts by classroom teachers to change their practices. The most interesting and lasting reform of the past decade will be the result of efforts made by educators who have been more concerned with what students are learning than about what teachers are teaching. As teachers, we found that designing for learning rather than planning for teaching demanded a different way of thinking about our work. As teacher educators, we have developed a method to help teachers be intentional about designing for student learning.

Our constructivist learning design (CLD) is based on the assumptions and processes of constructivist learning theory and offers a different way of thinking about learning and teaching. Just as reading and writing are intimately related, learning must be considered in teaching. These are two sides of the same coin. Many teachers have become aware of the pioneer work by Jean Piaget and Lev Vygotsky, psychologists who offered theories of constructivist learning. In brief, these men maintained that learners construct their own knowledge and that teachers don't just transfer knowledge to learners. Individual learners connect what teachers expect them to learn with their own experience. Learners engage in the social construction of knowledge. They make personal meaning for themselves, develop shared meaning with others, and then reflect on their meaning making in the public arena of the classroom. Piaget (1976) focused on the personal construction of knowledge in works such as *To Understand Is to Invent,* and Vygotsky (1986) emphasized the social construction of meaning with *Thought and Language.* They both accepted the intimate relationship of individual and interpersonal learning and recognized the power of "reflective abstraction" and "shared reflection." Reflection is a deliberate, self-conscious analysis of life experience. Reflection can be individual or collective; in either case it is a key to constructing knowledge.

Teachers who deliberately design learning activities so their students can make personal and shared meaning out of concepts, processes, and attitudes welcome the constructivist learning perspective. These teachers invite students to explain phenomena for themselves before examining experts' views or theories. Students work together developing their own ideas rather than merely accepting textbook summaries. When students then encounter experts' explanations and theories in original source material, they are better prepared to critically analyze those ideas.

One of the difficulties with constructivist learning theory is adapting it to classroom teaching. Making the transition from "expecting listening" to "supporting learning" demands that teachers examine their practice and reframe their teaching. Vito Perrone (1991b) reflects on how teachers will teach the way they are taught. He explains why it is difficult for teachers to change perspectives from "planning for teaching" to "organizing for learning." Most teachers' *images* of teaching have been shaped by years of being students. They learned about teaching by being participant observers for six years of elementary school, six years of secondary school, and four or more years of college. Their images of constructivist teaching are memories of teachers who engaged them in learning and encouraged them to think for themselves. Our CLD offers teachers an image of how to organize for student learning.

Need

Reform-minded educators expect students to solve problems, think critically about issues, communicate effectively, and relate well to others. These complex processes require an approach to learning that is much more than memorizing facts. The traditional system of education has often confused memorizing with learning. But being able to recall something does not mean that you understand it or know how to use it. Giving students information and testing their memory of facts does not offer opportunities to solve problems, think critically, communicate clearly, or work with others effectively. Receiving and remembering information does not engage students in learning. Landmark research by John Goodlad (1984) in *A Place Called School* confirmed that classrooms are often boring places for students. His teams conducted in-depth interviews with students, parents, teachers, and administrators in 13 triads or clusters of a high school, a feeder middle school, and a feeder elementary school. Hc found that about 90% of the time teachers tell students about information found in textbooks and then test them on memorized material. Students cited fine arts, physical education, and industrial technology courses as their favorites because they got to do something. Larry Cuban (1984) in *How Teachers Taught* described few changes in classroom practice throughout the 20th century. He found some interesting experiments in elementary schools, but most involved no more than one teacher out of five and lasted no more than a few years.

For most of the 20th century, educational practices have been driven by behaviorist psychology. The essence of behaviorism is that only observable and measurable behavior can be considered evidence of learning. Behaviorists assume that cultural transmission of knowledge rather than the personal construction of knowledge is the focus of teaching. School learning is presented as a process of operant conditioning based on a stimulus and response model with reinforcement of desired behaviors. As cognitive psychology has emerged during the second half of this century, more research and writing about rarely observable or measurable mental processes has occurred. Such mental phenomena include dreams, daydreams, mental images, emotions, values, beliefs, learning styles, and processes of thinking and reasoning. Acknowledgment of these mental processes is important if we are to make classrooms interesting places where students actively engage in learning and construct their own knowledge. Constructivists believe that knowledge is dynamic rather than static, a process rather than a thing, a pattern of action rather than an object. Seymour Papert (1993) encourages this movement toward "constructionism" and away from the "instructionism" of behaviorist psychology.

Perhaps *knowing* is a more appropriate term than *knowledge* to describe what results from learning. What we think of as a static "body of knowledge" has evolved over the centuries. First, the oral tradition is very fluid, and stories changed over time as they were passed on from one teller to another. Second, written language has changed enormously over time, and only a few scholars can translate early writing and thinking. Third, the paradigms of recent scientific thought are also shifting. One example in the past century is the movement in physics from Isaac Newton's laws to Albert Einstein's relativity theories to Niels Bohr's quantum mechanics to Murray Gell-Mann's quarks. The evolution of genetic biology during the same period demonstrates another paradigm shift as we moved from Mendel's identification of genes to microbiology to genetic engineering to cloning to mapping the human genome. In one century, our communications technology has moved from telegraph wires to telephone lines to transistors to microwaves to fiber optics to wireless cells to low orbit satellites. Even our laws, taxes, and codes change regularly with great political debate about the anticipated impact on society. Clearly what is considered knowledge changes all the time.

If knowing is a process of constructing meaning rather than of memorizing a body of knowledge, then our whole teaching strategy must be rethought. For education to emphasize learning rather than teaching, our role as teachers must change. No longer do we act as a sage on the stage but rather as a guide on the side. Instead of planning to teach a lesson by telling or showing, we should organize learning activities for our students. Teachers must have a clear image of knowing and learning from a constructivist perspective to appreciate our process design. By challenging some cherished beliefs about knowledge and learning inherent in our current system of schooling, teachers can move to a new paradigm for education. Teachers, however, must first challenge outmoded beliefs of the greater society in which they teach. What most people still expect students primarily to learn in school is a variety of processes. The three Rs of reading, 'riting, and 'rithmetic are certainly important but offer only a basic foundation for real life. Perhaps the real life Rs of a new millennium should be reasoning, relating, and recreating. Naturally, reading, writing, and mathematics are necessary to learn these three. There is just too much information to expect that students can be filled with a body of cultural knowledge as some have advocated (Hirsh, 1987). Instead of covering and memorizing a huge collection of specific information, students should know how to access knowledge when they need it.

We believe learning is a process of changing what you know by constructing patterns of action to solve problems of meaning. Confident that students can construct their own knowledge, teachers gain a clearer sense of what the word *education* means—to draw out rather than to put in. A teacher's role must then focus on organizing for student learning rather than planning for teacher telling. Because we believe that teaching can be a process of supporting learning, we offer our CLD as a way for teachers to think about how they can design for constructivist learning by students.

History

This book is for students of teaching, teachers, administrators, and parents who want to know how to apply constructivist learning theory in classrooms. Our CLD is the product of our ongoing dialogue with each other and with a host of teaching colleagues about ways teachers can organize for student learning. Both of us are teacher educators who have worked with new and practicing teachers in pursuit of master's degrees in education. We share a commitment to engaging students in learning when we teach. We typically arrange something for students to do that will get them thinking about a concept, process, or attitude we want them to experience. We frequently use original sources as assigned readings, draw from contemporary theory to frame our lessons, tell stories or anecdotes about teachers and students gathered from our experiences in schools, and write what students say on a board or flip chart to make their thinking visible and legitimate. We rarely read from a textbook, lecture from notes, or make presentations from overheads.

Our efforts to describe how we organize for learning have evolved into six elements: situation, groupings, bridge, questions, exhibit, and reflections. Each of these six elements represents an important process in constructivist learning theory in classroom practice. In teacher education courses, we share our process of organizing for learning with students of teaching to get their feedback and to see if they can use a similar process in their own planning. Students in math, science, and technology methods courses have used versions of our format to describe the themes they taught to elementary and middle school students. Many of them have appreciated our process of thinking about what students will do, and some have carried those ideas into student teaching and continue to use them in their own classroom planning. Experienced teachers in learning-community programs were very receptive to how we organized for student learning in these adult learning experiences. Many of them were motivated to teach by engaging students in learning rather than by telling them what they need to know, and they reported that the CLD process assisted them in organizing learning episodes that were consistently successful.

One of our focus groups described how they modified our CLD to meet their own needs. Some extended the timeline of one lesson for as much as two weeks, some used it for new lessons once every week or two, and others changed the order within the bridge and groupings categories to fit the way they preferred to teach (Gagnon & Collay, 1996). They were excited to have an alternative to the typical lesson-planning format that most districts use for evaluation. Because their principals saw a positive effect on student learning, they were willing to accept the CLD approach in lieu of a more traditional lesson plan.

Dilemmas

Many experienced teachers have taken risks with new approaches to learning and teaching only to be criticized by parents or administrators or to see their innovations swamped by the next wave of reform. We believe our CLD can be aligned easily with current thinking about standardized outcomes and goals-centered curriculum. The topic for each learning experience we organize is selected because our students want to learn it, because we feel it is appropriate to their development as teachers, or because we are required to teach it. As college teachers we confront the same dilemmas as constructivist teachers in elementary and secondary classrooms. How do we teach something that is developmentally appropriate or required so that students are interested, are engaged in active learning, and can demonstrate what they have learned? How do we address school goals, district outcomes, state rules or requirements, and national standards? How do we teach mandatory content so students find it interesting rather than boring? How can students become engaged in learning about key concepts, processes, or attitudes rather than simply remembering for a test what they have been told? How do students "show what they know" rather than take tests that are graded on the basis of what the students don't know? Our CLD offers a way to consider what should be taught and to use it as an opportunity to think about how students might learn concepts, processes, and attitudes. We reframe each topic as a *situation* for our students to think about and explain for themselves before they encounter the official explanation. We find that most students are interested in figuring things out for themselves, in working together to think about an explanation, and in sharing their thinking with others. As students listen to different explanations, they revisit their own thinking and confirm or reformulate their ideas. Our CLD provides a way to address the teaching dilemmas of balancing the required learning of education with the real learning of students.

An additional dilemma is presented by the use of educational jargon. We find ourselves questioning the accepted usage of some terms in educational writing, research, and standards. We deliberately use the phrase "concepts, processes, and attitudes" to convey different dimensions of knowledge. The accepted educational language described in current National Council for Accreditation of Teacher Education (NCATE) accreditation standards is "knowledge, skills, and dispositions." This implies that skills and dispositions are somehow separate from knowledge or are something different than knowledge. Is knowledge merely a collection of facts or information unrelated to what you do with it or how you feel about it? Perhaps some of the confusion derives from Bloom et al.'s (1956) taxonomy of objectives in the cognitive domain that begins with knowledge and proceeds through a hierarchy of comprehension, application, analysis, synthesis, and evaluation. Again, many educators accept his language as a standard. Bloom et al. later classified objectives in the affective domain and the psychomotor domain as well. This left us with a legacy of knowledge as separate from how we feel about it or what we can do with it. This separation continues in the 2000 draft of the NCATE standards that describes "What should elementary teacher candidates know and be able to do to have positive effects on student learning?" A common phrase in these standards is "Candidates know, understand, and use. . . ." This phrase implies that understanding and using knowledge are different from knowing something. We believe that what NCATE and Bloom et al. refer to as knowledge is really information and that the ways that learners construct knowledge for themselves may not be as discreet and hierarchical as Bloom et al. suggests. However, his classifications can serve as important guidelines for moving the goal of education beyond recitation of information. We contend that an understanding of education should begin with epistemology rather than with philosophy. Constructivist learning implies an initial concern with what knowledge is and how learners actively construct knowledge. Advocates of constructivism agree that acquiring knowledge is an active process of constructing meaning rather than a passive process of receiving information. For these reasons, we use the phrase "concepts, processes, and attitudes" throughout this book to represent different dimensions of knowledge or knowing.

Purpose

The purpose of our CLD is to offer teachers and students of teaching a way to think about organizing for student learning. If learning is a process of constructing knowledge, then teaching must involve supporting learners in ways that aid that construction. The teacher's role is to guide, facilitate, or coordinate learning rather than to dispense information. Our CLD offers a basic framework to help teachers think about organizing for learning by their students and to play out the basic processes of constructivist learning in the course of a lesson. It also incorporates assessment into each design element rather than isolating assessment as an end product or closing activity. The most important consideration is what teachers believe about learning. If they see themselves as telling students about the wisdom of the ages, then they probably don't agree with us that learners construct their own knowledge. Perhaps an example from teacher learning in real life will challenge their assumptions.

Think about your first year of teaching. Most first-year teachers report that they learned more that year about teaching than they had during their entire preservice experience. They also cite student teaching as the most valuable part of their teacher education. Much of what they learn is on-the-job training. They have to sink or swim in their own classroom using their own knowledge, interpersonal processes, humor, and mental agility. They must constantly keep their wits about them to survive. There is so much to learn. How do you manage 20 to 40 different personalities, sometimes five or six periods a day? How do you cover the prescribed curriculum in a way that interests students and keeps them actively engaged in learning? How do you assess individual learning and interpersonal processes? How do you communicate with parents? How do you keep up with changes in the profession and in your own field? How do you learn to remove yourself from the external world of adult interaction and community activity eight or nine hours a day? How do you learn to function in professional isolation without the benefit of working with colleagues or team feedback? The answers to all these questions lie in doing your own learning, constructing your own knowledge, and making meaning out of teaching for yourself.

Audience

The people who can apply our CLD to their work are experienced teachers as well as new teachers who are interested in organizing for student learning. They might be looking for another way of thinking about teaching, about applying the principles of constructivist learning theory in their classrooms, or about using a different format for lesson planning and evaluation. Some teachers already do many of these things with their students but have inconsistent results from lesson to lesson. Our CLD offers a consistent framework for thinking about basic constructivist learning processes that actively engage students in their own learning. We see our CLD being used in any classroom at any grade level and not only by teachers of math, science, and technology classes. We know a variety of teachers who use this way to organize for learning by their students: primary teachers in self-contained classrooms; intermediate social studies teachers in teams; middle school language arts teachers; high school physical education teachers; and specialists in art and music.

Staff development coordinators and school administrators also appreciate our approach to organizing for learning. Our CLD offers a framework for educators to consider as they seek ways to engage students in learning and develop assessment procedures to document that learning. Teacher educators can incorporate our CLD into a basic methods course in any elementary area or secondary subject. They can also use it with experienced teachers studying for advanced degrees and considering new ways of thinking about designing for learning. Parents who are engaged in home schooling or are active participants in their children's education will also be interested in CLD as a resource for thinking about processes of learning.

Scope

Educators are moving beyond teaching objectives that have easily measured outcomes toward accepting the multiple dimensions of knowing that occur in classrooms and in life. Constructivist learning theory emphasizes the processes of learning rather than the content or objectives of teaching. Theoretical assumptions about the processes of informal learning during life experience guide how we organize for formal learning in educational settings. In the first chapter we describe several theoretical assumptions about constructivist learning and map these assumptions directly into the elements of our CLD: situation, groupings, bridge, questions, exhibit, and reflections. Extended descriptions of how to organize for learning by considering these six processes make up the rest of this book. Each chapter describes one element in detail, gives specific examples from different grade levels and subjects, explains our thinking about each process and the related theory, and offers some historical precedents from prominent educators. We give some helpful "teachniques" for using these processes in teaching, and we provide practical considerations for you to think about with your colleague study group or learning circle as we did previously (Collay, Dunlap, Enloe, & Gagnon, 1998). Concluding remarks draw each chapter to a close. We hope you enjoy this journey through our approach to designing for learning!

Acknowledgments

We wish to acknowledge our teachers and our students. We have admired good teaching since we joined the profession as young adults, and we hope to model and teach our students in ways that will make our own teachers proud. Our teachers include mentors, who are great teachers: Pat and Dick Schmuck, Linda Lambert, Nathalie Gehrke, Diane Dunlap, Rob Proudfoot, Liz Wing, and Vito Perrone.

Colleagues who encouraged us in this endeavor and whose teaching we admire include: Kyle Shanton, Jan Lewis, Cathy Yetter, Sandra Gehrig, Valerie Lesniak, Sherry O'Donnell, Virgil Benoit, Christopher Dill, Helen LaMar, Joanne Cooper, and Gail Gallagher.

As teacher educators, we have worked with hundreds of teachers, and most of what we know about good teaching we learned from them. We have also worked with thousands of students who taught us about designing for learning.

In addition, the contributions of the following reviewers are gratefully acknowledged:

Merryellen Towey Schulz
Assistant Professor of Education, College of Saint Mary
Omaha, NE

Katherine Avila
Mathematics Teacher, Acton-Boxborough High School
Tewksbury, MA

Jeanelle Bland Hodges
Curriculum Specialist, University of Alabama
Northport, AL

Sandy Lofstock
Math Instructor, California Lutheran University
Thousand Oaks, CA

# About the Authors

George W. Gagnon, Jr. is a math models designer and math education consultant in Tacoma, Washington, who supports teachers in their classrooms to improve mathematics teaching and encourages the integration of technology in classroom activities. He has been involved in education for 25 years as a classroom teacher, school administrator, university professor, and community learning consultant. His interests include professional development, constructivist learning, communities of learners, and appropriate assessment.

Michelle Collay is Visiting Associate Professor at Pacific Lutheran University in Tacoma, Washington. A former music teacher, she is a teacher-scholar who seeks to improve teaching and scholarship in higher education and K-12 schools through collaboration with educators. Her research interests include new teacher socialization, school-university partnerships, and the creation of classroom communities. Her current research focus is on faculty socialization of women.

Introduction

Constructivist Learning Design

Education is a natural process spontaneously carried out by the human individual, and is acquired not by listening to words, but by experiences upon the environment.

—Maria Montessori,
Education for a New World, (1963, p. 3)

Teachers who embrace constructivist learning theory constantly seek ways to apply Montessori's insight in their classrooms. Many educators have deepened our understanding of constructivist learning (Brooks & Brooks, 1993; Fosnot, 1996; Lambert, 1998). They have described their theoretical assumptions about constructivist learning and have offered principles for applying this theory in teaching and in administrative practice. Our work with prekindergarten through Grade 12 teachers has shown us that many of them already use a constructivist philosophy in designing classroom learning experiences for students. Few teachers, however, can articulate ways to design for student learning or produce consistent results. After 10 years of organizing our own CLD for engaging students in active learning and of reviewing planning experiences with teacher colleagues, we can now describe a replicable process for applying CLD consistently.

When we refer to a *learning episode* we refer to a distinct learning event that is part of a larger learning event or is one of a series of learn-

1

ing events. In the next section, we describe how individual learning episodes, based on the same CLD, played out for the teaching team of Ellen, Gail, and Sue. This team of three middle school, language arts teachers designed the episode for several of their ninth-grade classes that were studying different genres of literature. They present an exemplary CLD learning episode.

Fairy Tales Learning Episodes

Ellen, Gail, and Sue had discussed designing a constructivist learning episode to introduce the elements of fairy tales to each of their ninth-grade classes. For homework, they had asked their students to write essays about personal experiences with fairy tales. On the day of the episodes, the teachers each opened class by describing her own experiences with fairy tales.

Ellen, for example, related the story of her Irish grandfather who had told her about the "little people" and had made them seem so real that she would look for them in likely hiding places. Next, students offered their personal experiences with fairy tales. Then Ellen asked her students to arrange themselves in groups of four and directed each group to list the common elements in fairy tales and to develop a definition of what made a story a fairy tale. Each group wrote its list and definitions on a transparency, presented it to their classmates, and explained their thinking as Ellen debriefed them.

Meanwhile, in another classroom, Gail had her groups of four students share their personal experiences with fairy tales and collect large chart paper, markers, and tape. She asked them to develop their own definitions of a fairy tale and to identify the common elements in fairy tales. Her students met for about 15 minutes of discussion while Gail moved among groups and asked or answered clarifying questions. She directed them to tape up their charts on the wall and to explain to their peers their definitions and the common elements they had identified. Gail invited her students to discuss their choices and their rationale for each choice.

In a third classroom, Sue first told a story about how she had enjoyed hearing fairy tales read aloud when she was a small child. She asked her students what they remembered about fairy tales as listeners, readers, or storytellers. She had them meet in writer's workshop groups and asked them to compare their personal experiences with fairy tales, to make lists of common elements in fairy tales, and to agree on a definition of a fairy tale. A student reported on each group's work, and Sue led a discussion in which students compared the different elements and definitions they had created.

In the next phase, each teacher handed out articles by experts who had defined fairy tales and listed their common elements. The three teachers asked their students to read the articles and then to compare and contrast their own definitions and lists with those of the experts. After 10 minutes, each teacher led a discussion of students' observations and reflected on how group definitions and elements were similar to those formulated by experts.

Finally, in each classroom, the teacher asked the students to answer two questions for the next day: (a) What would you add to your group's definition and list based on ideas from your peers and from the experts? and (b) Whose definitions are more meaningful to you in preparing to write your own fairy tale?

At the end of the day, the teachers talked together about how their learning episodes went. They spoke about the level of student engagement and about how collaborative thinking seemed so much more meaningful than in earlier episodes when they had lectured about the elements of fairy tales. They identified some students who seldom participated in the day-to-day activities of class yet who were excited about offering ideas to their small groups based on their own experiences with fairy tales. The teachers also talked about the importance of capturing the students' new knowledge in ways that documented their individual grasp of this area of literature. Ellen, Gail, and Sue had high hopes that their students were now prepared to write interesting fairy tales.

Figure I.1 is the "Fairy Tales CLD" or framework of elements they used to design their constructivist learning episode. In this book, we explain how to use this framework in designing for learning.

Learning Happens

Teachers can use constructivist processes to frame learning episodes around people, places, products, and phenomena. They can design

FIGURE I.1

Fairy Tales Constructivist Learning Design

Level: Middle School
Subject: Language Arts
Title: Fairy Tales
Designer: Ellen, Gail, Sue

Situation *50 minutes*	The purpose of this *situation* is to engage students in analyzing fairy tales so they develop an understanding of core elements and common themes that define this area of literature. Students consider their previous experience with fairy tales, develop their definition of a fairy tale, and identify a list of common elements that are found in fairy tales.
Groupings *5 minutes*	A. Students put themselves into groups of three or four. B. The students are provided with large sheets of chart paper, markers, and tape so they can write their group's definition of a fairy tale and list of common elements in fairy tales and post these for the exhibit. Copies of articles by experts defining fairy tales and listing common characteristics of fairy tales are given to individual students after the exhibit.
Bridge *10 minutes*	The teacher describes personal experiences with fairy tales and asks students to read what they have written the previous day about their personal memories of fairy tales.
Questions *15 minutes*	Students organize into groups and get paper, markers, and tape. They develop their definition of a fairy tale and list common characteristics of fairy tales. What were your previous experiences with fairy tales? How would you define a fairy tale? What are common characteristics of fairy tales? How do your definitions compare with the experts'? Were your definitions and lists as precise? After seeing the other groups' and reading the experts' definitions and lists, what would you add to your own? Which definition was more meaningful to you and would be more helpful in writing your own fairy tale? Why are we studying fairy tales? Where did fairy tales come from? What are fairy tales from other cultures?
Exhibit *10 minutes*	Student groups tape the chart papers with their definition and list of common elements on the white board and present their thinking to the rest of the class.
Reflections *10 minutes*	Students read the articles and discuss the similarities to and contrasts with their own definitions and lists. Then they write about what they would add to their definitions or lists from other groups or from the article. Students describe why their own definition or an expert's definition was more meaningful to them as they think about writing their own fairy tale.

learning episodes to engage students in constructing their own understanding of real learning events. The topic of study should be accessible in a variety of ways, opening many possibilities for the learning episode to be a real-life learning experience for students. Constructivist learning theory suggests that students become engaged in formal school learning just as they participate informally in learning during life experiences outside of school. Let us give an example:

> Think about how you learned to ride a bicycle and consider ours. Our experiences were similar but different. One of us had training wheels on an old Schwinn. The other used a pass-around bike that was virtually indestructible. The second bike was short, with hard rubber tires; it circulated through the neighborhood for use by children who were learning to ride. Both of us had had tricycles so we already knew how to pedal. One of us was the oldest child, so the parents had to buy the first bicycle in the family. The other was a youngest child, so all the older kids had bikes of their own. Both of us remember a lot of ceremony around learning to ride. We both pestered our family to get us a bicycle of our own. Training wheels were a great comfort and gave us confidence. They also gave us a sense of what it felt like to balance on two wheels with the security of outriggers in case we faltered. Parents were there to help put the training wheels on and to take them off when the rider was ready to solo. For learning to ride, we both received a lot of support that included verbal directions and encouragement, holding of the bike by an adult running along behind, expressed concern when we lost our balance, and expressed satisfaction when we balanced by ourselves.

The important point is that the experience of learning to ride a bicycle is deep knowledge—something that we could still do after not having ridden for thirty years. Our parents and brothers were teachers, but they couldn't do it for us. We had to learn to ride a bicycle ourselves.

Real-life learning and thoughtful school learning leave us with the same kinds of deeply internalized lifelong knowledge. In the case of riding a bike, although adults gave us a lot of support and guidance, we constructed our own patterns of action for balancing the bicycle and turning the pedals at the same time. We had to feel what it was like for ourselves. Even a great description could not give us the knowledge we needed to learn about riding a bicycle. Our knowing, then, was in doing the task ourselves and constructing our own pattern of action.

With CLD, the student creates knowledge instead of consuming information. Students want to learn and will risk making mistakes and even taking some falls in order to succeed. When others tell them or show them how to ride a bicycle, they choose what advice to take. When students learn to read, write, and do arithmetic, their experience is very much the same as when learning to ride a bicycle. Young children are very excited about learning basic processes if information is offered in a compelling way. Once engaged, the struggle is worth their effort, and they are much more likely to accept coaching about reading, writing, and figuring. If they aren't engaged, then teaching can be a difficult proposition.

We make the following assumptions about learners engaged in real-life learning events:

- Learners think individually to make personal meaning of learning events.

- Learners think collaboratively to make shared meaning of learning events.

- Learners connect their prior knowledge and previous experience to learning events.

- Learners pose questions and respond to questions about learning events.

- Learners present their thinking about learning events to others.

- Learners reflect on their collective and individual thinking during learning events.

We believe that these assumptions about learning through real-life experience can also be the foundation for school learning episodes. Each element of our CLD addresses one assumption about the process of learning during real-life events. School learning is most powerful when it clearly parallels real-life learning. The next section is an overview of how to design constructivist learning episodes by using these six elements.

Elements of the Design

The constructivist learning design we developed emphasizes six distinct elements: situation, groupings, bridge, questions, exhibit, and reflections. Figure I.2 is the simple template we use to arrange the six elements in a sequence that promotes and organizes our thinking about designing for student learning. Figure I.3 depicts the relationship among the six elements.

The *situation* is a comprehensive overview of the learning episode with a clear statement of your purpose and of the task you expect your students to accomplish as they make meaning of the event. The details of the learning episode unfold chronologically through the other elements. We continue with *groupings* of students and materials and move to a *bridge* between prior knowledge and current learning. We frame *questions* that teachers or students will ask as they think together about accomplishing the task. After students accomplish the task to the teacher's satisfaction as well as their own, they create an *exhibit* of their work. Then the teacher arranges for collective and individual *reflections* on their thinking. The students are the focus of the learning episode as they think together about how to accomplish the task.

Various considerations arise while designing each of the six elements:

1. *Situation.* What is the purpose of the learning episode you are teaching? What do you want your students to take out the door? How will you know your students have fulfilled your purpose? What task are you going to arrange for your students that will fulfill this purpose? How will you describe this task—as a process of solving problems, answering questions, creating metaphors, making decisions, drawing conclusions, or setting goals?

2. *Groupings.* Groups depend on the situation you design and the materials you have available. Address several questions to organize groups of students and associated materials:
   a. *Students.* How are you going to group students to think about accomplishing the task? Will they be grouped as a whole class; as individuals; or in collaborative thinking teams of

FIGURE I.2
Constructivist Learning Design Template

Level:
Subject:
Title:
Designer:

Situation	
Groupings	
Bridge	
Questions	
Exhibit	
Reflections	

FIGURE I.3
The Relationship Among CDL Elements

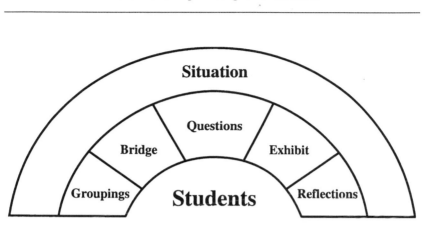

two, three, four, five, six, or more? What process will you use to group them randomly or intentionally? Will they count off, choose a favorite color or fruit, group by similar clothing or shoes, or by heights or birthdays? Do your want more sophisticated, teacher-selected groupings based on personalities, academic strengths, or students' choice of topic? We discourage "ability grouping" because school-defined ability can separate students into higher and lower status groups.

b. *Materials.* Do you want students to be engaged in physically modeling, graphically representing, numerically describing, or individually writing about their collaborative thinking? How many sets of materials do you have, and how many students can work with each set? What physical layout and furniture do you have, and how many student groups will you form? How are you going to distribute the materials to groups of students?

3. *Bridge.* What activity will you choose to determine students' prior knowledge and build a bridge between what they already know and what they might learn by accomplishing the task? Will you have the class solve a simple problem, define terms, play a game, construct lists, or discuss the topic?

4. *Questions.* What questions will you generate for each CLD element? What guiding questions will you use to introduce the situation, arrange the groupings, and set up the bridge? What clarifying questions will you use to understand student thinking and sustain active learning? What anticipated questions do you expect from students, and how will you frame responses so you encourage them to continue thinking for themselves? What integrating questions will you use to prompt exhibits and encourage reflections?

5. *Exhibit.* How will students record and exhibit the artifacts they created to demonstrate their thinking as they were accomplishing the task? Will students write a description on index cards or on poster paper and give a verbal presentation? Will they make a graph, chart, or other visual representation to present? Will they act out or role play their impressions? Will they construct a physical representation with models to show their thinking? Will they make a videotape, an audiotape, or use photographs to display their thinking?

6. *Reflections.* How will students reflect on what they thought about while they accomplished the task and while they watched others present the artifacts of their thinking? How can you lead the students in considering their collaborative thinking and reflecting on collective learning? What did students individually remember about the *feelings, images,* and *language* of their thoughts? What attitudes, processes, and concepts will students take out the door? What did students learn today that they won't forget tomorrow? What did they know before, what did they want to know, and what did they learn?

Precedents for
Constructivist Learning Design

Renowned educators like John Dewey, Maria Montessori, Paulo Freire, Eleanor Duckworth, Theodore Sizer, and Maxine Greene have advocated for similar elements. Educators worldwide are challenging themselves to heed the advice of these experts and to design for learning rather than plan for teaching. None of the ideas we present are new—we have just organized the thinking of many scholars of teaching into a framework that is sequenced and accessible. In addition, we discovered that researchers working directly with schools have identified patterns of planning for teaching that are similar to the writing and thinking of these scholars.

Several wonderful examples of how the constructivist process works in learning episodes are available from the Annenberg Foundation videos on teaching math in North America or the TIMSS videos of Japanese classrooms (National Center for Education Statistics, 1998). International conversations about constructivist learning address the importance of accountability. Some argue that learning episodes designed to meet national standards or curriculum outcomes can't really be constructivist. However, the concepts, processes, or attitudes selected as the purpose of learning episodes are only as significant as the teachers' thinking about them. Our students are engaged in active learning by thinking together, thinking critically, communicating their thinking, representing their thinking, and reflecting on their thinking. Most standardized tests are not designed to measure this kind of learning, but these processes and attitudes are consistent with contemporary international standards required of a global education for the new millennium. Many states have adopted assessment frameworks that try to evaluate higher-level student knowledge.

A brief history of modern lesson planning often begins with Ralph Tyler's (1949) *rationale* for the underlying reason for shaping curriculum. While his thinking was complex, acknowledging both the importance of a grounding philosophy and of the matching processes required to educate, he is best remembered for his ideas about measurable objectives. Tyler believed that teachers could not teach effectively unless the curriculum was well defined and learning objectives were specific and measurable.

Robert Gagne (1985) also described the difference between the education needed to learn simple tasks and the education required to learn complex tasks. He suggested that instruction should be structured to involve problem solving and to ensure higher levels of understanding. He introduced a focus on *learning outcomes* instead of on objectives. Gagne specifies nine relevant instructional events that vary with specific content and the type of learning outcome achieved: (a) gaining attention, (b) telling learners the learning outcome, (c) stimulating recall of prior learning, (d) presenting the stimulus, (e) providing learning guidance, (f) eliciting performance, (g) providing feedback, (h) assessing performance, and (i) enhancing retention and transfer to other contexts.

James Block (1971) offered the field of education *mastery learning*. He believed that knowledge was acquired on a continuum from simple to complex and that instruction should be structured to reflect this belief about knowledge. He collaborated with Bloom and others and used his hierarchy of educational objectives with *knowledge* at the bottom of the ladder, representing facts and figures, and *synthesis* at the top, representing the most complex action by the learner.

Such *instructional programming* frameworks emerged from an era that Case (1996) called the "cognitive revolution." This philosophy suggests that teaching behaviors and student learning can be structured and measured, from the most simple to the most complex. In contrast, constructivist learning theory focuses on the development of individual personal meaning, group shared meaning, and the collective construction of knowledge. With this philosophical framework, teaching becomes a process of bringing prior knowledge to the surface, actively engaging students in new learning, and connecting the two for as many students as possible.

Teachniques for Building Community

We coined the term *teachniques* to describe our suggestions for teaching techniques that you might use as each element of CLD unfolds in a learning episode. In other words, we make suggestions for guiding learning based on our experience about how CLD moves from a static design to a dynamic learning episode. We find these teachniques helpful in our own teaching as we move from planning to implementation. Perhaps the most important initial step is for teachers to intentionally set about building community in their classrooms. Richard and Patricia Schmuck (1997), two of our mentors, have taught a generation of educators their strategies for creating community in classrooms.

Humans learn in the company of others, and therefore, designing for constructivist learning must anticipate directly and specifically the role of other humans in the group. We have interviewed many teachers who are using our CLD. They all report the necessity of building community in their classrooms first, to create trust between teacher and students and among the students. The constructivist learning approach asks students to take risks by giving answers or by explaining their thinking before they know what the *correct* response might be. They learn by discussing their thinking with the class, and sometimes they expose misconceptions or make mistakes before considering reasonable explanations for concepts with the class and teacher. Being vulnerable out loud is different from most conventional exchanges between teachers and students and causes students to resist a more open-ended learning experience.

Most students have several years of experience playing the school game. They realize that to play the game well, they must "give the teachers what they want." Usually this means giving the "correct" response to a question from the teacher. The right answer typically requires students to speak about something they read in the text or heard in a lecture. They generally respond by recalling information rather than by articulating their original thinking. If their answer is correct, the teacher praises them, but if it is incorrect, they are often embarrassed in front of their peers. To risk being wrong or to suffer the embarrassment of exposing flaws in their thinking is not easy for people of any age. Most students' school careers have been spent minimizing this risk, so asking them to go against custom and to trust one another calls for a major change in their attitudes and self-concepts.

It takes time to build the self-confidence necessary to risk exposing one's thinking to peers. This confidence, however, is very important for teamwork, for effective communication, for problem solving, and for critical reflection. The attitude of confidence in one's self and trust in one's peers needs to be learned as does any other educational concept or process. Teachers must modify the classroom culture from competition to collaboration or students will not take these risks. Activities intended to build a sense of community in a classroom are very important if teachers are to succeed using the CLD. We have described several community building teachniques in our previous work (Collay, Dunlap, Enloe, & Gagnon, 1998).

Teacher Learning Circles

Like students who may be unfamiliar with a different style of learning and teaching, teachers also need encouragement and support as they engage with their students in CLD. It is essential that teachers work with colleagues to design for learning. Whether working on school or district reform or with a grade-level team or department to design curriculum, several heads thinking together are usually better than one reflecting alone.

Most teachers seek trusted colleagues' ideas and support in response to a mandated change such as standardized testing. Moving from a conventional method of lesson planning to a student-centered learning design like ours also requires special support and interpersonal interaction. Such support focuses on linking curriculum and teaching content with student presentations of thinking. Reliance on textbooks as the curriculum is limiting because most experienced teachers draw from a variety of content sources for ideas and materials. Recent movement toward national and state standards narrowly limits what textbooks are acceptable for a curriculum. The CLD supports efforts to focus on how students will engage with whatever curriculum teachers either are mandated to teach or choose to teach.

Here are some ways teachers suggest gaining support from colleagues. You need to determine which of your colleagues is interested in working with learning designs. As you would with any reform, choose colleagues who are genuinely interested and who will advocate for you and your ideas, not those who disagree philosophically. We refer to these collegial study groups as learning circles.

Choose a short time period of one to four weeks for learning circle experimentation so that you can maintain the energy required for change and can lower the feelings of risk that often accompany reform efforts. Schedule regular meetings (during a set preparation time or before or after school) to compare notes, share materials, and get advice about strategies or techniques that have been effective.

Build on both individual and team strengths, and don't abandon effective facilitation of student learning that has worked before. Always start with content that is familiar and necessary rather than tackling new content, new assessments, and new designs for learning in a single effort. Teachers we interviewed build on their strengths as they add new dimensions to their practice and do not leave behind methods that have proved successful.

Agree on a time or times to review your efforts and to get feedback from colleagues about how the unit or curriculum worked for them. Invite the principal or a trusted colleague from outside your learning circle to observe your efforts. Determine which aspects of the unit worked well and which need modification or change. Use innovative assessments such as portfolios to reassure yourself and your team about student learning.

Choose a curriculum focus that is central to your learning circle and that members are compelled to do well. Like the three middle school teachers described earlier in this chapter, come to some agreement on the key aspects that students are expected to learn. If you choose a required content or assessment as your focus, then prioritize those aspects most likely to succeed, and start with the most certain point on your list. Think together about how you will evaluate student learning and how you will educate administrators and parents about the ways in which your design supports district and community goals.

We are often asked how student learning is assessed in a constructivist learning episode. We see assessment taking place continuously and becoming integral in every element of the learning design. The challenge for teachers is to frame assessment procedures so they can be reassured about meeting unit, course, or state outcomes and about using their data to inform their constituents that students are learning.

To think about designing an appropriate learning episode, teachers arrange a *situation* based on their assessment of students' development, learning, interests, needs, and styles. They also develop a strategy for *groupings* based on their assessment of individual students' personalities and of how they interact with peers. Teachers make an initial assessment of what students already know as a *bridge* to what they want students to learn. They also need to create and anticipate *questions* to assess students' understanding of the attitudes, concepts, and processes that they are trying to learn from the episode. Another important assessment of how students think during a learning episode is the *exhibit* that they present for peers. Student *reflections* about what they have learned from the episode are also the basis for a self-assessment of individual learning. In most cases, these assessments can easily be aligned with external standards.

Concluding Remarks

We have worked with many teachers who have embraced our version of constructivist learning design as well as with those who have not seen it as appropriate for their classrooms. Math and science teachers often find this approach suitable for their subjects. Language arts, social studies, and fine arts teachers have also used this process to design engaging learning episodes for their students. Teachers from almost every grade level and subject area, including physical and special education, have discovered that CLD can be useful. We encourage you to use the six-step design process and see how your students respond.

The next six chapters discuss each element in the CLD. The *situation,* or the overarching theme that is central to learning design, is presented in chapter one. The other five elements follow in subsequent chapters.

Chapter 1

Developing Situations

The only true education comes through the stimulation of the child's powers by the demands of the social situations in which he finds himself.

—John Dewey, *My Pedagogic Creed* (1974, p. 427)

Our constructivist learning design (CLD) seeks to satisfy Dewey's pedagogic creed. The situation element aligns formal school learning with the "only true education" of real-life learning in social situations. This first element of CLD focuses on organizing learning episodes with specific purposes that stimulate students' powers through the demands of social situations. We say *learning episode* rather than *lesson* because we focus on learning that students will do rather than on teaching that we will do. In our typical learning episode, the teacher presents a challenging task for students to accomplish, supports students in thinking together about doing the task, asks them to explain their thinking after completing the task, and guides them in reflecting on their process of thinking and learning as they did the task.

This chapter describes the first element of our CLD, which we call the *situation*. We considered such terms as *problem, experience, event,* and *phenomenon* before settling on *situation*. A situation involves selecting a purpose for the learning episode and arranging a task for students to accomplish together that will fulfill this purpose. This task could be a problem to solve, a question to answer, a decision to make, a metaphor to create, a conclusion to draw, or a goal to set. We begin our CLD with this element because the most important question for teachers to answer is, "How will I arrange a challenging task for students to accomplish that fulfills my purpose?"

Characteristics of a Situation

A *situation* is a purposeful task for students to accomplish by thinking together. A situation should be challenging enough to engage the interest of most students and to actively involve them in making meaning for themselves. A situation should also be developmentally appropriate for students so that it corresponds with the outcomes or objectives for the curriculum at their grade level. And, in response to Dewey's pedagogical creed, a situation should be related to a "real-world" context as much as conditions of the learning episode permit.

The characteristics of a situation are these:

- It fulfills a specific purpose

- It presents an open-ended task to accomplish

- It compels interest by challenging students

- It is developmentally appropriate for most students

- It connects student learning to real-world experience

Each of these characteristics is important for you to consider when arranging a productive situation. We explain each characteristic more extensively so the significance is clear.

A situation fulfills a specific purpose. When experienced teachers design a learning episode, they first think about what they want their students to do. They often refer to such an event as an activity or a project. So we recommend that teachers start to design for learning with the following questions:

■ What is your purpose for the learning episode?

■ Why will students fulfill your purpose?

■ What will students take out the door?

■ How will students show what they know?

Once these questions are answered, it is much easier to think about the task that you want your students to accomplish. Usually your purpose centers on learning a particular concept, process, or attitude. Often that purpose is your own construction, a synthesis of several different expectations described in textbook objectives, school themes, district outcomes, state requirements, or national standards. You should state the purpose as clearly and simply as possible with words such as *understand* or *explain* or *express*. Your experience with the class and your familiarity with the content will let you decide why your students might be interested in fulfilling your purpose. Does the situation relate to their youth culture or apply to events in their lives?

Then you should determine what your students will take out the door that would fulfill your purpose. What are the key concepts, processes, or attitudes you expect them to learn? Next, decide what data from students will show you what they know and convince you that they have fulfilled your purpose: What do they need to produce as evidence of their learning? In the language of constructivist learning, your answers are *constructs* because you construct your own meaning about the purpose of a learning episode and about how students will fulfill your purpose.

Teachers who ask sophisticated questions such as these create purposeful learning episodes. A clear purpose challenges students to learn in the same way that real-life learning events do. Choosing a purpose before designing for learning will promote deeper reflection and analysis and give you confidence in your decision making.

A situation presents an open-ended task to accomplish. A productive situation is not a group of questions with right answers. A situation may entail a single task that students need to accomplish. Just as teaching is both art and science, there is artistry in designing for learning so that the task may be accomplished in many ways. More useful learning takes place when students think through ways to accomplish an open-ended task than when they memorize one *right* way to do a task. How will you frame the task to accomplish as a problem to solve, a question to answer, a decision to make, a goal to set, or a metaphor to create so that the students will take out the door what you want them to learn?

For example, teachers could ask primary-level students how many combinations of two numbers they can list that will total 13. This question has many answers and offers a variety of different ways to approach the task. The possible approaches range from a simple answer, such as $8 + 5 = 13$, to a complex answer such as $136 - 123 = 13$. Other possible answers include $12 + 1$, $11 + 2$, $10 + 3$, $9 + 4$, $8 + 5$, $7 + 6$, $14 - 1$, $15 - 2$, $16 - 3$, $17 - 4$, and so on. Students could show these combinations with base ten blocks, Cuisenaire rods, Unifix cubes, Popsicle sticks, straws, or any other manipulative model at their disposal. This task is open-ended and is more challenging for students than memorizing any single combination such as $8 + 5 = 13$. Open-ended questions are appropriate at every level.

Intermediate students learning Logo programming in a computer lab could be asked to construct the largest possible equilateral triangle on their screens. Middle school music students could be asked to develop their own clapping or drumming rhythm and to annotate it so that others could reproduce it. Another middle school example is asking students to identify a collection of 20 heights that would produce an average height of 5 feet 4 inches rather than asking them to average 20 heights. High school students might be asked to identify *all* stakeholders in the American Revolution, including not only the British, French, Dutch, and other Europeans but also the Native Americans, Spanish Americans, and African Americans—and then to determine the different perspectives of these stakeholders.

None of these open-ended tasks has a *right* answer. Each group of students can think about and explain their answers so that others can decide whether or not they are appropriate and accurate solutions to the task.

A situation compels interest by challenging students. Situations should represent big ideas that are worthy of consideration and require collaboration to accomplish. Students must engage in learning as members of a community rather than as individuals competing for the highest scores. Many students are turned off by competition between individuals to give *right* answers with speed and accuracy. Teachers can organize students, big ideas, and classroom space to develop a challenging situation that requires collaboration. When students work together to accomplish a task, they think and learn in a different way. Making meaning with other students is more compelling than working in isolation. If teachers can convert the content that students are expected to learn into a challenging task to accomplish, then students are more interested. Content includes concepts, processes, and attitudes that become part of the thinking needed to accomplish a task. Such tasks challenge both students and teachers to gain confidence in their ability to learn and teach.

A situation is developmentally appropriate for most students. Choose the next lesson from your curriculum or textbook and ask your students to develop their own ideas about it. For example, what does democracy mean to students? What is the right to vote and why is it important? How do they see people in their lives exercising their voting right? How could they find out if people vote or don't vote in their own community? What inventory or survey could they develop to understand why people do or do not vote? A primary teaching concern is, of course, that learning episodes must correspond with outcomes or objectives of the curriculum at particular grade levels.

Open-ended questions offer students of varying abilities a point of entry into the task to be accomplished. More sophisticated students can opt for more complex responses, whereas less sophisticated students or those who are more challenged learners can work productively at different levels. Students with limited reading ability, for instance, can draw a graphic representation of the answer or describe their ideas in a story. As they accomplish such tasks, all students improve their social interaction skills and gain self-confidence while learning.

A situation connects student learning to real-world experience. If you want students to explain what friendship means to them, there are several ways to connect it with their life experiences. They could script and perform a short play, write an essay and read it on videotape, record on audiotape the comments and opinions of peers, create a visual metaphor for friendship, or make a list of what they expect from a friend during tough times. They can determine what might be a good test of friendship, create criteria for being a friend, list words that are attributes of a friend, or decide how far they would go to save a friend's life. They could debate whether they would donate a kidney to a friend. The students might read some classic works on friendship and decide if those characters meet the criteria that they used in making their decisions.

A *situation* is a single task with a definite purpose that can define the entire learning episode. The other elements of the CLD merely help you think about the important processes for an effective learning episode and how it might unfold chronologically. Experienced teachers grasp the notion of a situation easily, but preservice teachers have a more difficult time understanding the concept well enough to frame a situation. They have a harder time seeing it as a comprehensive learning episode that begins with a single question or task that might be answered or accomplished in several different ways. Structuring learning to allow for diverse answers remains a challenge for experienced teachers, but such an open-ended learning event can terrify beginners. We suggest designing tasks first for more open-ended student learning in content areas where one has the greatest confidence. In any event, the teacher is *not* required to have all the answers before proceeding!

Examples of Situation Elements

In this section, we offer examples of a situation in four CLDs. They are taken from a dozen designs in the Resource section. These designs address four different levels of students. The primary (K-3) CLD example is from fine arts and is about drawing animals. The intermediate (3-6) example is from science and is about moon view. The middle school (6-9) sample is from language arts and is about fairy tales. The high school (9-12) illustration is from social studies and is about international trading partners. We chose examples from four different subjects to emphasize the utility of the CLD. Review these four examples of a situation and note that each includes a purpose and a task. Then consider how each example aligns with our list of characteristics. Are these situations open-ended? Do they compel interest? Are they developmentally appropriate? Do they involve use of prior knowledge? And are they connected to real-world experience? Compare the following examples (Figure 1.1) to these characteristics and decide whether or not each situation element satisfies our criteria. After comparing these four examples, refer to the complete designs in the Resource section to see how they condense a CLD.

FIGURE 1.1

Example Situation Elements

Situation 50 minutes	**Primary Grades: Fine Arts—Drawing Animals** The purpose of this sequence of three *situations* is for young students to make further meaning of the rhythmic, patterned story *Brown Bear, Brown Bear, What Do You See?* "Brown bear, brown bear, what do you see? I see a yellow duck looking at me." They engage in rich literature activities by listening to the story or song, drawing new animals, writing a parallel phrase, acting out new behaviors, describing these new behaviors in words, and retelling the story through new pictures and words. Students choose a new animal and a color for that animal. Each individual or group creates a page for a book about new animals. The teacher or assistant collects the sheets into a book and has students write on their page the story pattern for that new animal and color.
Situation 90 minutes	**Intermediate Grades: Science—Moon View** The purpose of this *situation* is to provide investigation of a basic science concept rarely understood by adults and often explained with misconceptions relating to shadows of the earth on the moon. Students work in groups to determine the relationship between the sun, the earth, and the phases of the moon. Each group is asked to explain their thinking through a diagram.
Situation 50 minutes	**Middle School: Language Arts—Fairy Tales** The purpose of this *situation* is to engage students in analyzing fairy tales so they develop an understanding of core elements and common themes that define this area of literature. Students consider their previous experience with fairy tales, develop their definition of a fairy tale, and identify a list of common elements that are found in fairy tales.
Situation 6 weeks	**High School: Social Studies—Trading Partners** The purpose of this *situation* is for students to investigate how global trade will influence their future employment. Students explore international trade between continents and determine how it might affect their future jobs. Teachers can specify region, goods or services, and jobs, depending on the required curriculum. The students list jobs of family and friends then review the want ads to see the kinds of positions that employers are seeking to fill. Students choose an occupation and company for the duration of the unit, then list ways it is linked to international trade.

Theory

Our CLD entails teaching for purpose rather than teaching to objectives. Teachers who use it already understand that; they also believe in the rationale of engaging students in a situation and understand what students will do with their new learning. Such a teaching strategy involves more than stating an objective to be learned or an outcome to be demonstrated. The situation embodies a purpose in creating a learning episode for students. Most CLDs are built around a big idea and often have multiple purposes. Teachers can't predict or limit what students will learn while engaged in an open-ended activity, so it can be difficult to focus only on specific, measurable outcomes. CLD purposes are usually more global than are objectives, and they involve introducing, exploring, or understanding concepts or ideas rather than demonstrating one particular behavior.

Educators were seduced by the behaviorists into thinking that narrowly specifying what should be learned and then testing for specific objectives would make learning more likely to occur. But experienced teachers realize that what we expect students to learn is not necessarily what they do learn, especially when there are more than 30 students in a classroom. The likelihood that they will learn increases, however, if the students are engaged and interested in a situation presented by teachers. Broad purposes that involve defining, experiencing, and investigating create authentic and transferable learning. In contrast, narrow pursuit of specific objectives that have been predetermined by a district curriculum or by officially adopted textbooks is less likely to produce optimal learning.

Vestiges of behaviorist thinking appear in current notions that concepts are static, that they can be described objectively, and that they can be learned in the same manner by all learners. For example, if the fourth-grade curriculum introduces fractions in mathematics, curriculum designers assume that all fourth graders will meet the objective of adding and subtracting fractions. They also assume that by following the textbook instructions, most teachers will successfully teach students to add and subtract fractions. The objective is for students to demonstrate, by answering test questions, that they can manipulate the algorithms and obtain a correct answer. Such a measurable objective can be reached by some of the students. What isn't known from such behaviorist practice, however, is whether students have a conceptual understanding of how fractions work even when they obtain a correct answer. Nor is it known what the students who give incorrect answers know and can do with the concepts. Unfortunately, teaching to an easily measured objective perpetuates the myth that clear objectives lead to good teaching. The number of high school students who still cannot add and subtract fractions demonstrates that this behaviorist strategy is flawed.

In practice, we know that different children learn differently, make meanings of concepts in different ways, and learn at different rates. Yet the same teacher who knows this truth about learning may also believe that an objective that has been defined is an objective that can be reached. This way of planning for teaching is so ingrained in most of us that it's hard to step back and challenge it.

So what kinds of thinking will provide teachers with the courage to move toward CLD? The first step is putting aside the notion that concepts are tangible objects that can be transferred from one person to another through explanations. Paulo Freire (1970) called this the "banking" model of education, where teachers make a deposit into students and expect them to give back the funds on demand. We approach teaching in another way: We think about knowledge as the *patterns of action* constructed personally by students who make their own meaning. We do not think about knowledge as *objects* that can be transmitted in neat little packages from teachers to students. The role of the teacher is to light a candle rather than to fill a piggy bank. Teachers who embrace the constructivist philosophy have moved beyond dispensing information and have entered a partnership for learning with each student. Recognize your own relationship with learning and make sense out of your journey to understanding. Creating a situation is much more than setting up an opportunity to experiment with ideas—it represents your values, beliefs, and dreams about your place in the world. Education is a complex social process of human interactions about meaningful ideas.

Most teachers consider three main areas when they plan a lesson, and these areas are depicted here as a teaching plan triangle: expectations, evaluations, and materials. We have represented these in Figure 1.2. The sides of the triangle represent the components of a static lesson before it is taught: expectations, evaluations, and materials.

Expectations are the base of the triangle and encompass the continuum of national standards, state requirements, district outcomes, and teacher objectives for the lesson. *Evaluations* include the typical tools for determining student learning from the lesson, such as homework, quizzes, exams, and regional, state, or national standardized tests. *Materials* include the resources available for teachers to use with that lesson, such as textbooks, teacher manuals, anthologies, articles, or curriculum guides. A common visual metaphor for these components is a three-legged stool. Perhaps this is an apt representation because many lessons are conducted as the teacher sits on a stool, has students read the

FIGURE 1.2
Teaching Plan Triangle

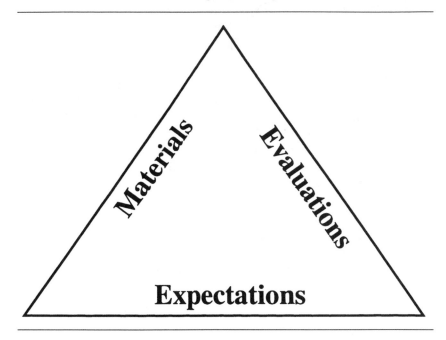

materials, explains the materials to the students, and then evaluates their understanding of the materials.

Modify this representation in your mind as you look at Figure 1.3. We have added a third dimension to the triangle—giving it a bottom to transform it into a learning design pyramid. The term *students* has been added to the design and occupies the base of the pyramid. The three sides are *purposes, assessments,* and *resources.*

You develop your own purpose for each learning episode as you derive meaning from all of the expectations bearing on your teaching. You decide on assessments to use throughout the learning episode—for example, profiles, portfolios, presentations, proposals, paragraphs, or performances. The resources for the learning episode include original source writings, physical models, graphic materials, community members, and technology. The students, who make up the foundation of the pyramid, can be viewed as individuals (including personality type,

FIGURE 1.3
Learning Design Pyramid

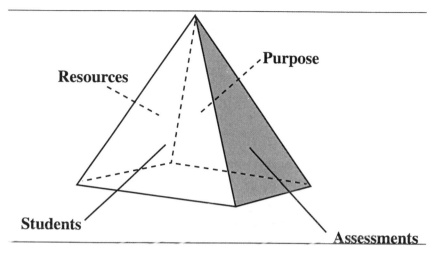

thinking style, and developmental level) or as a group (emotional, social, and discipline needs).

The learning design pyramid depicted in Figure 1.3 also represents the movement through time as these four factors interact and your constructivist learning design unfolds in a dynamic process of thinking and learning. When you unpack the learning design during a real-time learning episode, the art of teaching becomes central to your success as you use teachniques to move your learning design from theory to practice, from generic to specific, from ideal to actual. We hope this visual metaphor about arranging a situation for students is a teachnique that will support you in your transition from thinking to doing and from planning for teaching to designing for learning.

Precedents

John Dewey used the term *situation* in his essay *My Pedagogic Creed.* He focused on situating new learning in the natural world of the child. He described building on children's experiences in the home by continuing to recreate similar activities at school. He never portrayed education as the acquisition of a set of skills. In 1897, Dewey wrote "I believe that education must be conceived as a continuing reconstruction of experience; [and] that the process and the goal of education are one and the same thing" (p. 434).

Professionals best know Donald Schøn (1983) for his theories about reflection in action. He also conceptualized the situation in a very constructivist way. Like architects, educational professionals are challenged to solve problems in real-world situations rather than to merely apply theoretical rules to abstract problems. Experienced practitioners see a variety of situations in their work and bring a repertoire of problem-solving strategies and ways of thinking to each new situation.

Eleanor Duckworth (1987) described how to use situations to engage students in "the having of wonderful ideas" about science. She observed that when left to their own imagination, children would construct and reconstruct their own meaning of the world around them. Children's efforts to explain different situations result in creative, innovative, and theoretically sound understandings of the natural world.

Leslie Steffe and Beatriz Ambrosio (1995), researchers of constructivist learning, built situations for students to explain new understandings of math concepts. Catherine Fosnot (1996) invited several contemporary philosophers to write about their understanding of constructivism. In addition to chapters on the disciplines of science, mathematics, and language, she broadened the conversation to include the fine arts.

Maxine Greene (1995) provides examples of real-world learning from the fine arts. She thought carefully about how children create, interact, and learn to make meaning within the fine arts, reminding readers that children learn from experience, and experience should include interactions with the aesthetic side of life: "Where education is concerned, large-scale solutions hold little relevance for situation-specific undertakings. Local knowledge and local coming together ought to counter the tendency toward abstraction, as should a conscious concern for the particular, the everyday, the concrete" (pp. 68-69).

As we discussed at the beginning of this chapter, the tradition of creating or recognizing a situation to engage students in learning can be seen in all fields of study.

Teachniques for Situations

Good teachers have always drawn ideas from a bag of tricks, which they begin to fill early in their careers and add to over time. Our advice about teaching techniques, or *teachniques,* for setting up a thoughtful situation comes from our years of teaching experience; from observing good teachers; from the traditions of group process, cooperative learning, and active learning; and from freely trading teaching stories back and forth with others in various disciplines.

Framing Tasks as Real-Life Experiences

In a recent undergraduate Foundations of Education course, we asked a group of preservice secondary teachers to generate a list of activities they might use during the first few days of school to engage high school students. Their list was quite long and inventive, and many of them said the exercise was one of the most meaningful and useful that semester. They could also see the benefits of borrowing from other disciplines, something not typical of experienced secondary teachers. Among their suggestions for a situation were these:

- High school English students could ask family, friends, and neighbors about their favorite poem, favorite author, or favorite type of literature.

- Middle school social studies students could interview five members of different households and ask them how many people live in their house and how many television sets they have.

- High school fine arts students could examine three different kinds of clay pots—coiled, thrown, and pinched—and the tools used to shape the clay. Each student would then choose one kind of pot that she or he would like to create, speculate on the tools needed, and then experiment with clay to make a pot in the chosen style.

Deriving Rules From Examples

Another common approach to developing tasks is giving students several different examples and asking them to derive rules for classifying or determining patterns.

- Primary students could develop rules to sort a collection of buttons into different categories.

- Intermediate science students could examine several different rocks and develop rules to classify these rocks in distinct categories.

- Middle school math students could measure the circumference and diameter of several circular or cylindrical objects such as plates, bowls, clocks, cans, bottles, jars, or lampshades. By dividing the circumference by the diameter, they would produce a rough approximation of pi (3.1416) as the relationship between those two dimensions.

- High school foreign language students could look at several different examples of regular verbs in the present, past, and future tenses and determine rules for forming those tenses with new verbs.

Tweaking Textbooks

Textbooks can provide a sequence of study or of outcomes for teachers. Often textbooks reveal explanations before students have a chance to think about a topic for themselves. One way to tweak a textbook is to ask students to think about a topic before they read the textbook.

- Primary students could determine how many different ways there are to form a hexagonal pattern block—as an introduction to basic fractions.

- Intermediate social studies students scheduled to learn about India could begin with a world atlas and a topographic map of the country. Before reading the textbook for information about cultures, languages, dress, food, and other aspects of

Indian life, students could spend some time generating ideas about the climate. Over several sessions, they would first discern the characteristics of the climate and geography and then determine what cultural characteristics they'd anticipate finding in a country that has large, arid regions with few rivers or other sources of water. Information in the textbook will then be more meaningful.

- Middle school math students could solve as a group the problems in a chapter section before reviewing the textbook explanations or solutions.

- High school chemistry students could try to sort index cards that give pertinent information about individual elements into a rough approximation of the periodic table as an introduction to that topic.

Unpacking Assumptions

Our colleague Kyle Shanton adopted the constructivist learning design in his literacy methods courses. At first, his teacher-students resisted using his constructivist procedure. They saw it as more appropriate for math or science teaching because it seemed to be based on solving problems or explaining situations. With some experience, however, they could conceptualize ways to encourage students of literacy to engage in making meaning of story and language rather than in memorizing.

An example from Kyle's class involves modeling how to teach a certain story to young children. In the story, a young Mexican American girl tells about her neighborhood. Kyle asks the adult students to think about what young children might already know about their own neighborhoods, and the adults discuss this question. He then reads the first chapter of the story. After this chapter and each subsequent one he reads aloud, he takes time for conversation about the young girl's experiences. He invites his students to expose their assumptions about the girl and the culture in her border town and also how they might approach teaching this story. Kyle's thorough, step-by-step learning episode is designed to move students from liking or not liking a story to a much more reflective level of decision making. They have been challenged by this task to think like teachers who are mature and socially responsible rather than like students doing an assignment.

Learning Circle Considerations

This section, like a similar section in each of the five elements chapters that follow, is intended as a guide for talking with colleagues about your own professional development. We refer here to learning circles or collegial study groups. Begin your conversation by choosing a topic that you and your colleagues are expected to teach. Instead of planning how you will explain it to your students, design a situation so that your students will learn the topic by accomplishing a task. Frame your topic as a concept, process, or attitude. Have your students learn by trying to figure out a concept they don't already understand, by performing a process they can't currently perform or by developing a positive attitude toward something they presently feel anxious or uncomfortable about. In other words, engage your students in learning the topic by arranging a task for them to accomplish.

Examples of tasks include resolving an open-ended problem that may present several potential routes to solutions, asking and answering questions about how a proposed project might affect your community, creating a visual or graphic metaphor, making a difficult moral or ethical decision about ending or extending a life by organ transplant, drawing collective conclusions about how to restore a complex system to health, or setting appropriate task goals as individuals or as work groups. Some of these tasks are short activities, and others are long-term projects. The important idea is to challenge your students to think, to work together, and to learn something through their own initiative. Other ideas for tasks include scripting a skit or dialogue, developing a logo or advertisement, designing a structure or bridge, proving a theorem or corollary, documenting accomplishments in portfolios, defining a term or category, composing a piece of music, mapping a playground or school, using a magnetic compass to create regular polygons, drawing a continent or world map from memory, or communicating in sign language. Let your learning circle decide on a few things to try.

We believe that lasting change takes place only with the support of colleagues. Teachers are socialized into a way of thinking about learning and teaching. You could try CLD on your own, but we encourage you to find a group of colleagues who want to take responsibility for its own professional development. Talk with them about designing for learning. Such change is incremental and takes time. Don't try changing every subject or class right away. Try CLD as an ongoing classroom experiment or an action research project. Consider making a few small changes at a time. Use our CLD one day every two weeks or one period every two days until you feel comfortable with it. We have changed our teaching in many ways over the last ten years. Perhaps our most rewarding professional development came through dialogue about designing for learning.

As we described in the introduction, national or state standards, district outcomes or textbook adoptions, and school themes dictate the content of most curricula. Teachers shape school learning experiences so that the material becomes relevant and meaningful for students. Some textbooks are actually useful tools or are at least useful some of the time, but many are not. Textbook content and adoption should not limit the ways in which you frame the learning of children or adults. Ownership of a thoughtful situation designed to engage learners is one of the most powerful ways that you can take back the curriculum and reenergize your teaching.

For us, curriculum is comprehensive and subsuming. It includes all interactions between the teacher and students, not just the content of what is taught. We recently taught a curriculum development course for graduate students and asked them to bring an artifact of their curriculum to class. Of the 30 students, most of them prospective administrators, 28 brought in their district curriculum guide. Only 2 teachers brought examples of models intended to engage students or samples of student work. We designed a three-month task requiring our students to develop a case study of curriculum, including pieces such as interviews with curriculum directors, curriculum maps, assessment processes, and a CLD. Their curricular recommendations and presentations of artifacts on the final night of class demonstrated a broad interpretation of curriculum and served as a culminating assessment of understanding. The key to their success in rethinking curriculum was participation in a learning circle with other professionals whom they respected.

Concluding Remarks

The situation, as indicated by Figure I.3 in the Introduction, is an overarching framework that determines how the other elements of the CLD will unfold. We know that teachers are initially prepared to specify objectives, cover the mandated curriculum, and produce students who pass standardized tests. Many states today, however, evaluate student learning in comprehensive ways that require teachers to assess students differently. Whether teachers begin with the evaluation overview and work backward or choose key curriculum concepts from the year's offerings, our CLD is more likely (than traditional methods) to prepare students for the higher level assessments they now face.

The situation can be chosen to reflect your strengths and interests *and* to prepare your students to demonstrate their learning in ways that will make it evident to parents, administrators, and community members. To actualize a CLD is not to disregard the realities of schooling. You can ensure that certain topics or ways of knowing are experienced and practiced without relinquishing your personal values about learning. With the pressures of testing and evaluation more and more evident in schools, you can be easily discouraged about charting a high-quality course of education for your students. We hope our CLD's overarching situation allows you the freedom to build strong curricula and be confident in student learning.

Chapter 2

Organizing Groupings

The ultimate purpose of a teacher guiding a group of students through the different stages of development [in group process] is to maximize the learning ability of the individuals by developing group norms and procedures that encourage all students to do their best.

—Richard and Patricia Schmuck, *Group Processes in the Classroom* (1997, p. 6)

This chapter describes the next element of our constructivist learning design, which we call *groupings*. As the Schmucks suggest, how students are grouped and supported in working together to accomplish a task is central to designing for learning. It is the second process for teachers to consider in CLD.

Whole-class grouping is so common that we may not think of it in the *group* category. The teacher-to-students dynamic of a large class reflects certain familiar habits. Teachers who work primarily with whole-class groups may be making a conscious decision about how students learn or may be teaching the way they were taught. When teachers present to students as a whole group, question individuals within the group, and explain a concept to everyone at the same time, they are assuming that each student learns the same way and will make the same meaning of the information. Individual students may then work on their own to complete an in-class assignment or to get a head start on home-work. When students work in isolation or receive information as a whole group, the social construction of knowledge is not realized.

Small groups are necessary for students to move from personal meaning to shared meaning in the social construction of knowledge. We use a variety of different groupings to engage students in thinking together as they accomplish the assigned task. Students can be grouped in different ways depending on the purpose. The class can begin in one grouping and evolve to another. For example, the bridge is done with the whole class and then students are separated into small working groups based on topic or interests. Another time, the students might be put into groups first and then asked to work on a bridge. Whatever configuration and order of groups you decide to use, think deliberately about how the groupings will best serve your purpose for learning.

Public education for everyone is essential in a democracy. For indi-viduals to function well as citizens of a democracy, they must work effectively with others. Reports from the business community about their expectations for young employees identify the need for skills in problem solving, communication, and teamwork. Cohen (1994) described a group of sixth graders who refused to believe that adults often work together in small groups that include people who aren't their friends. Only when parents reassured them that this is true would stu-dents accept it. The emphasis we place on groupings in our CLD dem-onstrates for students the value of accomplishing tasks in learning teams or working groups.

There are also short-term groupings in which students meet for min-utes or for part of one class period to complete a short activity. Most often, these are *thinking groups.* In addition to offering students time to think together, such brief groupings allow teachers to observe different combinations of students. Ideas can be brought to the surface quickly and individuals can begin to think aloud. Early in the term, students need this time to get acquainted by learning names and finding out a lit-tle bit about one another. But short-term groups generally don't develop the level of trust or intimacy required for deeper or more risky learning.

We use the term *learning circles* for groups of learners, whether col-leagues or students, who work together over a longer period of time. Members of learning circles need to establish personal rapport and learn to trust one another. They support one another's learning through encouragement, constructive criticism, and realistic assessment of each person's work. A feeling of community develops between these students or colleagues as they interact, think together to accomplish tasks, and present their thinking to peers. We value these kinds of groupings because students and adults feel membership in a community of learners as they are actively engaged in learning. There are generally two kinds of learning circles that meet over time: a base group that is randomly configured and meets regularly throughout the term, and an interest group or project group that meets to complete a specific task. These groupings parallel colleague teams that teachers find in schools and that students will find in the workplace.

Many major dilemmas we face in society require analysis of complex systems and movement toward acceptable solutions. These dilemmas include disposal of nuclear waste, the lethal residue of conventional weapons such as land mines, the potentially destructive force of nuclear weapons, environmental contamination from toxic chemicals, ethnic cleansing and retribution, religious conflicts that erupt in wars and murders, economic disparity between the few rich and the many poor, and the worldwide population explosion. None of these problems will be solved without groups of people communicating and thinking together to create solutions rather than just taking sides and defending established positions.

In our own lives, all of us have addressed major problems such as conflict in a relationship, child-parent authority struggles, money income and outgo, emergency medical treatment for accidents, long-term illness of parents or children, structural home repair or improvement, and recovery from natural disasters. In addition, we face minor problems every day, such as, Where are the keys?; Who is going to take the children to day care?; What are we going to have for dinner?; How do we find reliable appliance repair service?; Where can a watch or VCR be fixed?; and Why won't the car start? Whether the challenge is major or minor, we often turn to our family or friends for support and advice as we try to figure out what to do. Sometimes just talking through a problem with others helps us sort things out. At other times, we need specific advice or suggestions because we are not sure how to proceed.

The value of working in groups to resolve real-life problems is undeniable. Most of us appreciate the support of family, friends, and colleagues when we need to talk things out. Moreover, many major corporations are organized into working groups or teams that accomplish particular tasks or goals. Corporate time and money is spent on leadership training and team-building activities designed to help employees become more comfortable working with one another and cooperating on a task. Complex problem solving in business, industry, science, engineering, law, and medicine requires a team of people with a variety of expertise. In education, the norm is still an individual teacher working alone in a classroom. Many teachers plan in grade-level or multiage teams in elementary schools or in interdisciplinary teams in middle schools, but they usually teach and solve problems by themselves. When teachers reflect with colleagues, they experience the benefits of learning together. As they realize the value of group processes for themselves, many teachers are encouraged to have their students learn together.

Characteristics of Groupings

Groupings organize students to accomplish the task framed in the situation and determine what materials they will use to explain their thinking. Groupings of students and materials are connected because the way students are grouped often depends on the situation you have arranged, the materials you have available, and the length of time these groups will be together. Groupings should be flexible and can range in size from dyads to a whole class depending on the purpose of the learning episode. The groups should be small enough to allow students with divergent thinking styles to talk together effectively but large enough to represent different abilities and diverse perspectives. Teachers should be deliberate in deciding how students will be grouped—randomly, by gender, ethnicity, or interest, or by some other criterion. The basic principle for groupings is that students work together to construct shared meaning.

The characteristics of groupings are these:

- Group configuration varies.
- Groups accommodate difference.
- Groups solicit thinking from all members.
- Groups account for individual learning.

■ Groups are organized deliberately by teachers.

■ Groups are assigned specific sets of materials.

Here, we examine the importance of each characteristic.

Group configuration varies. Teachers adjust the size and membership of groups according to the purpose of the learning episode, the materials available, and the length of time involved. Students should understand the purpose of the learning episode and imagine accomplishing the task. Most effective communication takes place in small groups of two to six students. Teachers can form random groups, or carefully assign students to create productive teams. Smaller groups of pairs or trios work well with younger students and teacher prompts such as "talk about this for a few minutes." Larger groups are better for older students and long-term base groups and for learning circles that stay together for a unit, month, quarter, semester, or year. When groups work together over a long term or on a large project in a learning circle, time allotted to the bridge and other elements may be extended.

Groups accommodate difference. There are some questions to ask when configuring groups. Are students clear about how a group will support their new learning? Students need to spend some time getting to know one another and talking about how they think and learn most productively. They might also need to describe the support they need from the group for listening, speaking, thinking, or writing.

Are members of the group well acquainted, or are they working together for the first time? This is important because group members will build trust by knowing one another's history, beliefs, and experiences. More time is needed for members to get acquainted when learning circles are new. Similarly, experienced learning circles can move quickly into complex tasks, although community building always requires informal reconnecting at the beginning of each session.

How will teachers assign group roles so that students engage in learning and develop social skills? We use the roles of convener, observer, recorder, and reporter for the students who initiate and monitor the group process and who record and report group thinking. We ask older students to make sure someone is attending to each role but assign specific roles to younger or inexperienced students. Sometimes we ask the youngest or oldest student or the student who has traveled the far-thest or the tallest person to be the reporter for the exhibit so that no students are left out of the task.

Groups solicit thinking from all members. How are students most likely to share their own thinking with one another? Conditions of trust and respect are important if everyone is to feel comfortable contributing his or her thoughts, particularly if they are unsure of themselves or their thinking. Students should be encouraged to explain what they are thinking and why. Articulating ideas might expose flaws and misconceptions, but it is important for students to understand and address this in the process of learning.

Groups account for individual learning. How will groups document their new learning? Many teachers are reluctant to use student groups because they can't adequately assess individual performance. A way to hold students accountable for their own learning is to ask them to explain other members' thinking. This assessment captures both group and individual performance. We ask all students to record group thinking and choose reporters randomly.

Groups are organized deliberately by teachers. What processes will be used to create groups? Teachers need to be clear about the size of groups, how groups are configured, and when groups are reconfigured. We use several approaches to form groups. These include the groupings that are listed here and then explained next: random grouping, limited-choice grouping, hand grouping, and student choice.

In random grouping teachers assign the students to groups by randomly distributing tokens. Tokens can be different colored index cards or handouts, colored paper clips, colored dots, or colored fabric. Other tokens include playing cards, stickers, chapter headings, cartoons, famous quotes, pieces of a puzzle, sentences of a paragraph, related words, or objects from the topic such as math models or different kinds of mammals. Shapes and stickers that represent the content are useful, such as squares, triangles, rectangles, and so forth, to make up math groups; notes on a staff to make up music groups; and the characters from a story for literature groups whose members will discuss their character's place in a story. Jigsaw pieces are terrific. We cut up political cartoons into five pieces each, have students draw them out of a hat, find the holders of the other pieces, and then analyze the cartoon. We cut up quotes or textbook headings and have these groups review their part of the text and share their findings with the rest of the class.

Limited-choice grouping is similar, but students have some choice about the group they join. If all the red dots go together, the students have no choice. If every group is required to have one of each color, students have some choice about where they go. Students of all ages will trade tokens. This used to bother us, but now we take time to watch who is trading with whom and take note of which students are uncomfortable working with new people.

Hand grouping is done in advance by teachers because they want a specific combination of students to work together. We advise against ability grouping and urge teachers to mix students by thinking styles, gender, ethnicity, experience with a topic, interests, high and low talkers, or age. If students are allowed to choose their own groups, a dynamic of popularity and exclusion can result. We use this method sparingly and only after trust is well established. Give yourself permission to regroup students at any time if personality conflicts or other dynamics impede progress. Some CLDs move through a variety of groupings.

Groups are assigned specific sets of materials. Often the best tasks have students use materials to model their thinking or track events in an experiment. For example, you can provide a prescribed set of commercial materials such as pattern blocks, instruments, topographic maps, or microscopes for the students to use in accomplishing their task. At other times you can use materials such as poster paper and markers for drawing maps, paints and brushes for creating a mural, jars of beans and rice for estimating—or balances made from rulers, string, and paper cups. The more that students use materials to make their own meaning, the more they will be actively engaged in learning.

Examples of Groupings Elements

In this section, we offer examples of groupings in four CLDs taken from a dozen designs that are in the Resources section. These designs address four different levels of students. The primary (K-3) CLD is from physical education and is about imitating animals. The intermediate (3-6) example is from media technology and is about Logo. The middle school (6-9) sample is from math and is about base blocks. The high school (9-12) illustration is from foreign language and is about Spanish songs. We chose examples from four subjects to emphasize the utility of the CLD. Review these four examples of groupings and note that each has a Part A for students and a Part B for materials. Then consider how each example aligns with our characteristics. Do these groupings vary by size, accommodate differences, support collaborative thinking, encourage accountability for individual learning, and specify arrangements for configuring groups and assigning materials? Compare the following examples (see Figure 2.1) to our criteria and decide whether different groupings of students and materials exemplify the characteristics we gave. After studying these four examples, return to the complete learning designs to revisit them in context.

Theory

We are guided by the principles of classic social constructivist theory. Vygotsky (1986) introduced the notion that learning is a social experience. Individuals thinking alone first make personal meaning. Then they test their thinking in dialogue with others to construct shared meaning. Finally, they construct collective meaning by reviewing shared meaning in a larger community. Movement through these three phases of meaning making embodies the process of socially constructing knowledge.

Thomas Kuhn (1996) describes a very similar process of socially constructing knowledge on a worldwide level in *The Structures of Scientific Revolutions*. He explains how many exciting theories in the past century were first proposed by individuals, then debated by groups who studied the theory, and eventually accepted by the international scientific community. Examples include the theory of relativity, quantum mechanics, plate tectonics theory, theories of contagion and vaccination, and the standard model in modern physics and chemistry. Most of the problems facing the world today are complex and do not have simple solutions. Teams of people working together nationally and internationally conduct research to find solutions. Current examples are the inter-

FIGURE 2.1

Example Groupings Elements

Groupings *1 minute*	**Primary Grades: Physical Education—Imitating Animals** A. Students work in the same small groups as in the Drawing Animals learning design to create actions for their new animals. B. They need space and clothes for free movement.
Groupings *10 minutes*	**Intermediate Grades: Media Technology—Logo** A. Students work in pairs determined by self-report of advanced and basic computer skills. B. Students work in pairs or in small groups on the computer depending upon how many are available.
Groupings *10 minutes*	**Middle School: Mathematics—Base Blocks** A. Students get into six groups by counting off from one to how many there are in the class. Then they divide their number by six and get into groups by remainders; zero, one, two, three, four, and five. B. Groups work with blocks that model a base that is two more than their remainder; remainder zero group works with base two, remainder one with base three, and so on.
Groupings *First day*	**High School: Foreign Language—Spanish Songs** A. Students are grouped based on the number of letters in their Spanish names. No group should be larger than 4. B. Each group needs a CD or cassette player and a computer with Internet access.

national research on cancer and on HIV and AIDS, the human genome mapping project, and the elaboration of string theory in physics.

We subscribe to the constructivist theory of Jean Piaget (1976) and his notion of active learning. We also believe that students do better when they think together in groups, record their thinking, and explain it by presenting an exhibit to the class. As they actively engage with others to think together, they become more interested in learning. The power of the group for learning was well documented by John Goodlad (1984) in his extensive study of schools.

Members of a group are more excited about learning if they work with materials or models to explain their thinking. They are engaged physically as well as mentally and make their thinking visible for others. Students who progress more through their feelings and images than through language benefit most from such hands-on, minds-on learning experiences. The movement from personal meaning to shared meaning making is supported when students construct a physical representation of their thinking. Some students use the models to show their thinking, and others give form to their thinking by handling the materials.

The materials category is often included at the end of lesson plans as an afterthought rather than at the beginning as an early consideration. We have seen many teachers dismiss lessons or activities because "they don't have those materials in our school." Other teachers feel that math models or science equipment is not developmentally appropriate for older students, even those in intermediate grades or middle school. Yet we have seen many adults engage in fascinating discussions about how to arrange a set of colored wooden blocks to demonstrate their thinking about a mathematical concept. We have also seen middle school students whose eyes brighten when they use materials to construct a metaphor or clarify a presentation for classmates. The use of concrete objects is considered unnecessary by some who expect students to work with abstract ideas only. Students, too, will try to dissuade teachers from the use of learning materials, declaring, "Those are for little kids!" Do persevere. The clarity and visibility of thinking is enhanced when students move beyond verbal explanations to a physical representation of their thinking. The prospects for useful, real-world assessment increase greatly.

The materials or models themselves have great power to affect the group members' learning. Give a group of people something to handle and play with, and wonderful sharing and talking about learning can emerge. For instance, when math students collaborate to physically represent an abstract idea, their handling of models creates a tangible connection between the learners. Another use of materials is for a writer's workshop, when teachers give students *realia* (real objects) to handle, to create metaphors with, and to write about. One of our favorites from professional development work is "basket of shells." Each person chooses a shell from the basket, sketches it, and writes about how she or he is like a shell. The students talk about the shell's shape and history, about its having been the home of a creature, about its having layers of calcium deposits and perhaps having spirals. Writers can then extend their understanding of themselves as growing life forms. The choice of materials that students use to accomplish a task by physical modeling, graphically representing, numerically describing, or individually writing about their shared meaning has a profound effect on the growth of the group.

Precedents

Many teachers are familiar with cooperative grouping in classrooms. You may have been introduced to this practice as a child, in teacher education coursework, or as a practitioner. Learning with others is not new, however, teachers who support cooperation rather than competition are often seen as radical.

The work presented by Roger Johnson and David Johnson (1998) in *Learning Together and Alone: Cooperative, Competitive, and Individualistic Learning,* by Robert Slavin (1983) in *Cooperative Learning*, and by Spencer Kagan (1990) in *Cooperative Learning: Resources for Teachers,* focuses on cooperating to learn. These authors challenge teachers to move away from dependence on individualistic learning models and toward cooperative learning models. Students learn content more comprehensively in cooperative groups. Social skills necessary for cooperative learning are taught proactively along with the cognitive focus. For example, each student gets a section of a book, chapter, or article and is responsible for reviewing the information in that section and for teaching it to others in their cooperative group. Each student is then tested on the entire text. This jigsaw format, initially described by Elliot Aronson (1978), promotes resource interdependence yet acknowledges individual contributions. Students must learn and practice group facilitation by, for example, encouraging everyone to participate.

Robert Slavin (1987) uses a tournament format to challenge learning teams to be thorough and productive in a more competitive atmosphere. He presents student team-achievement divisions that blend competition and interdependence while supporting student learning of basic facts and information. Shlomo Sharan and Yael Sharan (1992), in *Expanding Cooperative Learning Through Group Investigation,* show how student learning and inquiry improve when aligned with cooperative learning traditions. Spencer Kagan reviewed Sharan and Sharan's work on cooperative learning in his comprehensive handbook for teachers.

Elizabeth Cohen (1994) in *Designing Groupwork: Strategies for the Heterogeneous Classroom*, and Mara Sapon-Shevin (1999) in *Because We Can Change the World: A Practical Guide to Building Cooperative, Inclusive Classroom Communities* focus on the importance of creating equity and establishing democratic classrooms or communities of learners. These texts stress the need to improve equity, access, and inclusion of all learners in the classroom. They pay special attention to issues of diversity and use cooperative learning to disrupt racist, sexist, and language-exclusive curricula.

Well-managed groupings within the framework of CLD are a powerful tool for changing the norms of unequal education experienced by girls and boys. Studies of coeducation and single-sex groups in classrooms and schools have been around for a generation. Myra Sadker and David Sadker (1994) raised the awareness of many teachers about sexism in schools. Constructivist curriculum offers girls and other marginalized groups of learners more equitable access to education. Resolving equity issues in all classrooms every day is a challenge, but our constructivist framework assists teachers in treating students equitably.

Researchers of bilingual education value the constructivist approach to learning and teaching. The focus on social interaction and cooperation improves learning for all students. English speakers also benefit from classrooms where every student is legitimized and no student is stigmatized. Virginia Collier (1995) and Stephen Krashen (1997) advocate grouping bilingual learners with English speakers. They focus on the importance of interactive cooperation between learners of both languages.

Richard and Patricia Schmuck (1997) describe using group process strategies in classrooms and schools. They focus on the tensions and possibilities of heterogeneous groups as members strive to find common ground. This struggle generates powerful learning about self, others, and organizations for both students and teachers. They often consult about organization development, using group processes for professional development of school staff, teachers, and principals. School personnel can be more productive members of site councils and other decision-making groups when they use group processes. And teachers can use the same group process strategies to support student learning.

Learning to use groupings effectively is central to constructivist learning and teaching. Because most of us were taught in large groups, we have few images of how small-group learning looks and feels. Keep in mind your real-life learning experiences—generally there are others around to support your learning. Seldom did you learn something new just by yourself. Teachers using cooperative learning groups have many resources including colleagues in their schools. One excellent resource to support teachers' learning is Celeste Brody and Neil Davidson's (1998) *Professional Development for Cooperative Learning: Issues and Approaches.*

There are many precedents for using materials to support student learning. Friedrich Froebel organized the first kindergartens in Germany during the mid-1800s. His "gifts and occupations" are beautifully described in Norman Brosterman's (1997) *Inventing Kindergarten: Nineteenth-Century Children, Twentieth-Century Art.* He described the value of materials for learning such as clay, blocks, and tokens. Maria Montessori designed specific materials for young children to investigate in terms of, for example, size, shape, length, weight, and sound. Many of these materials required children to order objects as they replaced pieces. Several of these materials are described in Dr. Montessori's own handbook (1965) and include pink cubes, brown prisms, sound cylinders, and musical bells. George Cuisenaire was a music teacher who designed a set of graduated color rods for his students who were having difficulty learning mathematics. In the mid 20th century, Zoltan Paul Dienes (1967) developed attribute blocks, rectangular and triangular versions of multibase blocks, and inscribed place value blocks that have been copied in many different plastic variations. These thinkers had a profound respect for the physical representation of thinking.

Teachniques for Groupings

Using group process or cooperative learning well in designing for learning is, at the same time, deceptively simple and exceedingly challenging. We advise teachers to start simply and work up to more complex groupings and tasks.

Committing to Using
Group Process or Cooperative Learning

Your commitment requires both basic social skills and sophisticated strategy. Sometimes teachers are reluctant to organize groups because they assume that their students are not able to work well in small groups. Both teachers and students may press for getting right to the lesson, and some may feel the time it takes to set up or work in groups is wasted. Many students and some teachers are not familiar with the social skills that are needed for interaction and that are further developed through group process. Students must be taught about teamwork and cooperation throughout their schooling, not just in kindergarten. Don't give up on students or on your ability to facilitate their work right away! Remember, the most important characteristic many employers seek is the ability to work with others. Students can learn collaborative strategies, and teachers can learn to teach them. The quality of collaborative thinking convinced us of the value of small groups in facilitating learning.

Random or Ability Grouping

Category A of groupings focuses on how you will organize students into groups as you engage them in learning episodes. We often randomly assign students to short-term groups for thinking and accomplishing tasks. We prefer groups of four or five because they are large enough to allow interaction among several students and small enough that most students feel comfortable contributing to the conversation. These groups generally stay together throughout the whole learning episode and then present their thinking about the task. Random grouping is perhaps the best way to equitably mix students and get a balance of ability, gender, ethnicity, or other demographic characteristics. Over time, this kind of random grouping usually ensures that each student will work with a variety of other students. Research suggests that this kind of heterogeneous grouping results in a positive experience for all students. When more academically successful students serve as coaches or guides to others, they come to understand the concept, process, or attitude addressed in each learning episode more deeply. The less academically successful students also have an opportunity to participate with their peers, to be challenged, and to contribute a different perspective to the group process. All students learn from socially constructing knowledge.

Using Materials to Make Thinking Visible

Category B of groupings focuses on materials that you will need for groups you organize. Sometimes, you may have only one set of materials and need to arrange a demonstration or a series of stations so each group will accomplish a different task. At other times, you may have enough materials for each student to work on an individual project. Most of the time, we have five to eight sets of materials. Rather than thinking about the whole class, we think about what four or five students will do with a given set of materials to accomplish a task. How can the group of students use the materials to demonstrate their understanding of a concept, show a process, or display their attitude about an issue? Materials can make student thinking visible to small-group members or to others during the *bridge* or *exhibit.*

Learning Circle Considerations

Many teachers are using groups in classrooms: cooperative groups, study groups, project pairs, or presentation teams are examples. Interesting topics for discussion in your learning circle include how to organize appropriate groups or how to use groups in different subject areas. Because teachers usually teach the way they were taught, teachers using small groups to engage students in more powerful learning may find themselves in unfamiliar territory. New teachers may experience group learning in high school or college, but their early socialization may not encourage group learning. Your learning circle can have productive conversations about the advantages and challenges of grouping students and about the benefits of heterogeneous and homogeneous groups. We often see teachers try to use groups in a classroom and give up after a few attempts because "These students just can't work in groups." When students are asked to learn in a different way, they may protest because their comfort level is disrupted. Learning together is a process that can be taught and practiced. Start with the simplest activity—*think, pair, share.* Then ask pairs to complete a very quick task, and afterward compliment them on the quality of teamwork rather than on the quality of product. Discuss the results with your learning circle and make plans for moving to groups of three or four students. Go carefully but deliberately, and your students will learn with you.

Concluding Remarks

Grouping students is not new in education. Committees, task forces, and working groups are common in extracurricular organizations but are seldom used in classrooms. Teachers who support learners through personal, shared, and collective meaning making will ask students to think together about what they are learning. We see random groups as very useful when a topic is introduced or early in a course of study. As teachers get to know the students, they can hand group them by personality, attitude, or work habits, mixing or matching these traits to create easy or difficult working conditions for students. This aspect of education acknowledges the human interactions involved in communicating, relating, and learning. Competence and humanity in social interaction are just as important to education as the subject matter or content to be learned. The way students learn life lessons can depend on the way they learn to work together and get along with peers during school. Teachers can no longer ignore the process of learning and just focus on the content. We encourage you to be thoughtful about how *groupings of students and materials* are formed and how those groups can successfully accomplish the task you have arranged as a situation.

Chapter 3

Building Bridges

We now understand that learning is a dual process in which, initially, the inside beliefs and understandings must come out, and only then can something outside get in. It is not that prior knowledge must be expelled to make room for its successors. Instead, these two processes—the inside-out and the outside-in movements of knowledge—alternate almost endlessly. To prompt learning, you've got to begin with the process of going from inside to outside. The first influence on new learning is not what teachers do pedagogically but the learning that is already inside the learner.

—Lee Shulman, "Taking Learning Seriously" (1999, p. 12)

This chapter describes the third element of our constructivist learning design, the *bridge*. This element is critical to applying constructivist learning theory in a classroom. As Shulman (1999) suggests, before beginning any new learning, teachers can surface the prior knowledge that students bring with them; it serves as the foundation for a bridge between what students already know and the new learning they will engage in during a learning episode. Students carry an array of information, and some misconceptions, about any topic that comes from such sources as the media, folk wisdom, and popular culture. Some students have bits and pieces of vocabulary, whereas others have complete definitions that are quite accurate. Sometimes no member of the group really understands the concept or can connect it to his or her life experience. A good example of this phenomenon is portrayed in a short video made at a Harvard graduation about 10 years ago by the Annenberg Foundation (Harvard-Smithsonian Center for Astrophysics Science Education Department, Science Media Group, 1987). Titled *A Private Universe,* the film shows graduates and professors alike, who were randomly selected and were asked to explain why there are four seasons. Most attributed summer to the period when the earth is closer to the sun in its orbit and winter to the period when it is farther away. Only 1 person in 20 accurately described the tilt of the earth on its axis as the reason for seasons. If teachers hope to organize effective learning episodes, they must find out what current perceptions, constructions, or misconceptions students bring with them. Teachers must understand what students actually know or think before introducing new learning.

Characteristics of a Bridge

A bridge may be short and sweet or long and deep. It doesn't need to be exhaustive, but it should be adequate for the depths of knowledge within each learner. A good bridge makes that knowledge available to the teacher and classmates. Traditionally, the opening activity, or anticipatory set, was designed to set up a lesson, not to find out about prior knowledge. The bridge must link existing student knowledge to new learning. The design of a bridge will determine the quality of the new learning, so it must be thoughtfully planned and documented.

The characteristics of a bridge are these:

- It surfaces students' prior knowledge.

- It refocuses students.

- It organizes students into collaborative groups.

- It builds community between students.

▓ It creates a shared understanding and vocabulary.

▓ It gathers information about what each student knows.

Each of these characteristics is an important part of building a supportive bridge between what the students already know and what you want them to learn. We will explain each characteristic in more detail.

A bridge surfaces students' prior knowledge. All students benefit from the chance to review prior knowledge as they learn new things. Students can connect prior knowledge with new learning to make both more meaningful. Some teachers shy away from lengthy public descriptions of current knowledge because they fear that articulated misconceptions will get in the way of correct understanding. They hope to reduce the weight of excess baggage that students bring with them to the learning episode. Such efforts to bypass existing knowledge, however, allowed Harvard graduates and some Harvard faculty members to retain misconceptions throughout their very expensive educations. We encourage mining any and all conceptions for several reasons.

First, all students, whether youngsters or adults, are honored by the assumption that they already know something. A learning episode that begins with something they know is much more interesting than the usual message that "here is something else you need to learn about."

Second, most student and adult conceptions contain elements of *truth,* and those elements can be the basis for building new learning. Students are better motivated to pursue new learning if they can be convinced that their existing knowledge is legitimate.

Third, teachers and students together weave a tapestry of understanding when all are encouraged to bring their ideas forward. Ideas can be rewoven in gentle ways that take advantage of existing ideas in the construction of new ones. This evens the playing field so that those who always have the right answer no longer dominate the public domain. Often, the nonreader or the emotionally difficult child makes the most colorful contribution to the weaving. The group's old and new knowledge then includes contributions from all students rather than merely being a presentation of expert knowledge.

Fourth, old ideas will not just go away without some discussion. Whether fully formed or half-baked, they will continue to lurk in all of us. The good and the bad carry equal weight in our minds and hearts. The final product will be more comprehensive and deliberately formed if initial understanding is given its place in the development of the new learning.

A bridge refocuses students. When students come into the classroom, the teacher needs to get them to refocus or to move from one subject to another smoothly. This is especially important for secondary teachers who face students moving from room to room or from subject to subject every hour or so. Elementary teachers, however, face a similar challenge when creating a transition from recess or lunch to a topic of inquiry or from one area of study to another. The difference between telling students to open their books to page 43 and having them write or tell a neighbor something they know is evident in their body language, willingness to engage, and attention to one another.

A bridge organizes students into collaborative groups. The bridge can be created in a whole group, in small groups, or by individuals. Many teachers begin with a whole-group discussion about the learning that will be constructed or that will become *the construct.* For the secondary teacher who has 45 to 55 minutes, the advantage of a large-group conversation is efficiency in revealing data about existing knowledge. The disadvantage is that some teachers ask a few students to give their opinion and then assume that they represent the group. For many students, the whole-class format may not be conducive to offering their ideas. Shy students or those with misunderstandings are least apt to contribute. A more effective technique is to have each student write down one response in a notebook or on a card. Teachers can call on individual students for sample responses or collect and review the cards.

Groups are very useful during a bridge. These groups are usually randomly composed and small enough that each person can speak in the time allotted. For example, if a teacher only wants to allow three minutes, the dyad is the obvious choice. If a bridge involves setting up a longer unit, and the groups are predetermined by interest or topic assigned, then groups of three to six are appropriate. Most students discuss their thoughts more easily with a small group of peers than with the whole class. We often see just a few students engaged in class discussion, but when we ask the class members to turn to a neighbor or talk with people at their table, there is a buzz of activity and ideas. That is one reason we place the bridge after groupings in our CLD.

A bridge builds community between students. Building a bridge together also provides an opportunity for students to form a new working group, become familiar with peers, and get comfortable with any new procedures. Using groups to do a bridge usually takes more time than having a whole group discussion, but we feel that the time is well spent. As we move around from group to group and sample their conversations, we have a better understanding of how individual students think and of what roles they might play in the group. This window of opportunity for community building will pay big dividends in improved relationships, more respectful interactions, and a greater appreciation for different kinds of learners, especially those poorly served by the "fastest is best" kind of choral response.

A bridge creates a shared understanding and vocabulary. Teachers can make use of the language their students bring into a classroom by creating opportunities for each learner to define what she or he means by a certain word or idea. Teachers can also encourage two or more students to agree on a definition, but they must allot time for students to develop a thorough understanding of important concepts. By building a bridge, teachers defy the adage of ineffective teaching, "I covered the subject, but students didn't learn it." As teachers and students become familiar with what they already know, all are better able to make connections with new learning. When students are in small groups, they can work together on a minor problem or question. This activity serves as an introduction to the topic and also gets students thinking about what they already know. The bridge can employ a puzzle, a game, a definition, a brief explanation, or a list of characteristics.

A bridge gathers information about what each student knows. This characteristic of a bridge will influence the rest of the learning design in several ways. First, individual student assumptions and knowledge about the topic are exposed. Second, the quality of interactions between members of a class becomes apparent. Third, baseline data or pretest information is gathered and reviewed by class members and the teacher. Fourth and finally, steps leading to a main task are more certain because the pathway of previous learning has been illuminated. The quality of the instruction can be modified to take advantage of accurate and inaccurate student knowledge and can be linked directly to student interest. For instance, students can be grouped by interest and yet still be expected to learn about the same topic.

Examples of Bridge Elements

In this section, we offer examples of a bridge from four CLDs taken from a dozen designs that are in the Resources section. These designs address four levels of students. The primary (K-3) CLD is from reading and is about retelling *Brown Bear.* The intermediate (3-6) sample is from special education and is about vending machines. The middle school (6-9) example is from industrial arts and is about scooter motors. The high school (9-12) illustration is from business education and is about creating spreadsheets. We chose examples from four subjects to emphasize the utility of the CLD. Review these four bridge descriptions and note that each involves the students in activities intended to find out what they already know about the topic of the learning episode. Then consider how each example aligns with our characteristics. Do these bridge activities surface students' prior knowledge, focus students on the topic, organize students into collaborative working groups, build community between students, create a shared concept base and vocabulary between students, and gather some information about what each student knows? Analyze which of these characteristics are included in the following examples (see Figure 3.1) and decide whether each different bridge satisfies enough of our criteria. After exploring these four examples, review the complete designs to see how they fit into the flow of the whole CLD.

Theory

Finding out what students already know about a concept, process, or attitude you want them to learn is a basic principle of constructivist

FIGURE 3.1
Example Bridge Elements

Bridge *12 minutes*	**Primary Grades: Reading—Retelling Brown Bear** The teacher shows the pages of the new book. Children try to remember where their animal went and what it ate after seeing another animal. Teacher and children brainstorm and chart words that tell how each animal moved, where it went, and what it ate.
Bridge *10 minutes*	**Intermediate Grades: Special Education—Vending Machines** The first part of this *bridge* focuses on breaking down a five-dollar bill into smaller denominations and counting the money. The second part of the *bridge* includes a whole-class visit to a vending machine area so that each child or young person can put coins or paper into a machine, get at least one product out of the machine, and retrieve any change.
Bridge *First week*	**Middle School: Industrial Technology—Scooter Motor** Each team of two to three students is given a part of a small engine. Looking at a schematic, they must identify the part, describe its function, and tell which other parts it interacts with. They might also examine the part to see if it is in good condition or worn and in need of replacement.
Bridge *First day*	**High School: Business Education—Creating Spreadsheets** The teacher hands out index cards and asks students to put down anonymously the amount of money they get and spend each week. Then the teacher tallies these results with the class and discusses what categories might be used to present this information. For instance, under $20, $20 to $39, $40 to $59, $60 to $79, $80 to $99, and $100 or over. Then the teacher creates a spreadsheet with the tallied information and draws a chart showing the distribution. Teacher and students brainstorm the possible categories of income and spending: food, clothing, entertainment, transportation, games, computers, books, or sports.

theory. Whenever we encounter something new, we make sense out of it by connecting it with something we already know. Our young child talks about building cranes or backhoes "resting" or "sleeping" when they are not working. He also recognizes that a movie or television show is over when the credits roll. So when commercials for discount CDs of popular hits during past decades come on and song titles scroll down the screen, he is convinced that a show is ending and turns it off (to our delight). As adults, we also build on what we already know to make sense of new experiences.

As teachers begin a constructivist learning episode, their first step is finding out what their students already know or think they know about what they are going to learn. Sometimes students know much more than we expect, and at other times they have a great deal of misinformation. Either way, we are better prepared to support their learning if we understand what they already know or think about a concept, process, or attitude. We taught a learning episode on fractions many times to prospective teachers in elementary math methods. The bridge question is about what the top number and the bottom number are called and what each means. Usually the words *numerator* and *denominator* surface quickly. When we ask about why those terms are used, the students speculate freely about numerating and denominating. Few students have ever described the bottom number as denominating the total number of parts in the whole and the top number as numerating the number of parts designated by that fraction. The balance of the learning episode is spent investigating wholes and parts with the purpose of clarifying this relationship.

Piaget's (1976) notion of "disequilibrium" between existing schema and current experience, as well as Vygotsky's (1986) idea of scaffolding to support students in building new learning on old, are the classic constructivist interpretations of the impact that prior knowledge has on new learning. We experience the world based on what we already know and believe. New experiences are perceived through the lenses of old knowledge, so individuals will make different meaning from the same event based on their prior knowledge. We view the bridge as an important initial assessment for the teacher. Teachers can take a quick inventory of what students already know to decide how the learning episode should proceed. They get a sense of what knowledge most individuals bring with them and what the class in general understands. This assessment can be helpful in deciding which groups to spend more time with or how to modify a task for different groups. Sometimes we have to change our whole approach, as in the circumference lesson when we realized that students did not understand what pi was or how it was derived. Understanding that derivation became the topic of our next lesson. The basic idea is that you might want to test the water temperature before jumping in. Don't assume that you are aware of what students already know at the beginning of a learning episode.

Precedents

All lesson-planning schemes attend to beginnings and endings, which generally fall into two camps—external and internal control over learning. An example of the external way of thinking about learning is evident in the work of Dwight Allen, who introduced the concept of *microteaching* in the 1960s. His teaching represented a systems approach to teacher education that trained teachers to display certain behaviors he had linked to student learning. It called for videotapes of lessons that were then analyzed for the presence of eight steps. The student teacher would reteach the lesson based on feedback from this analysis. The first of eight steps was called a *set* and required the teacher to "set-up" the new lesson, sometimes by asking the students what they remembered from a previous lesson and sometimes by stating facts or giving information. Although that strategy was an improvement over the one expressed by, "Open your books to page 47," it provided the teacher with little useful information about the learners in the class.

Madeline Hunter's (1980) *Mastery Teaching* was a guide to help teachers improve their lesson planning. Although teacher preparation and inservice were shaped by her work for over a decade, teachers often spoke critically about being "Hunterized" by their districts. Her efforts to describe a common language for teacher planning and instructing were heroic if behaviorist. These methods of full-group instruction, however, did contribute to teacher lore. For example, she offered teachers strategies for assessing individual attainment of concepts. This improved on the inadequate full group dipstick method that depended on the choral responses to questions such as, "Does everyone understand?" or "Who can tell me about . . . ?" Although this method elicited some student knowledge, it was often limited to knowledge that could be reported quickly.

Both of these approaches reflect the work of Robert Gagne (1965) and David Ausubel (1968). Gagne suggested a system of nine instructional events that began with these three: Event 1 was "gaining attention," Event 2 was "informing learners of the objective," and Event 3 was "stimulating recall of prior learning." The third event was focused on asking students to recall any relevant prior knowledge. Ausubel suggested using an "advanced organizer," described as a verbal or graphic overview that abstractly relates new concepts to previous learning. Related concepts are graphic organizers, structured overviews, pretests, timelines, directed reading lessons, and directed viewing lessons. All of these methods assume external control over learning as teachers try to force a fit between new content and what their students *should* already know. This approach also deprives students of their internal control over learning, their responsibility for learning, and their work connecting new learning with prior knowledge.

Internal control over learning is a better fit with our CLD. We assume that students not only have prior knowledge about a concept, process, or attitude but that students also will differ in how they make meaning and construct new knowledge. Your initial assessment during a bridge should elicit individual student knowledge, assumptions, values, beliefs, and motivation to learn more about a topic. Your bridge should also give you an indication about how and when to move into the situation task that you will give students during the learning episode.

Teachniques for Bridges

This section extends the bridge metaphor with other ideas about connecting prior knowledge and new learning.

Engineering Bridges

We are often amazed at what students already know about the content of a lesson. They have a variety of learning experiences from inside and outside the classroom. Taking time to find out what some students know and what others don't know can surface valuable resources for all students. Identify the students who can be encouraged to coach others. They might need some subtle suggestions to help other students understand what they know instead of just telling them about it. They can also serve as resources by explaining key concepts to others in their group. We also encourage you to have a backup activity or extension question that will engage groups who finish their explanation quite quickly. Be sure to have students explain their thinking to you. Then redirect their explanation or prompt further thinking. We encourage you to engineer bridges for your own situation.

People Bridges

Doing the bridge in small groups gives students an opportunity to meet peers who are not in their usual social groups and even to form new friendships. Many students feel more comfortable speaking up in small groups and participate more fully in the bridge activity than in larger groups. The small-group format also lets you observe the interactions among group members before the situation task is addressed. Your observations can give you valuable information about the strengths and weaknesses of group members and about how different students relate with each other.

Floating Bridges

We live on Puget Sound in Washington. Several inland bridges do not arch over a body of water but instead float on the surface. Elsewhere, military engineers construct floating bridges that can be dismantled and moved along with the troops as needed. Our notion is that a CLD bridge also floats and can be dismantled and moved. If you are already familiar with what your students understand, then surfacing prior knowledge to connect with new learning might be accomplished quickly. In that case, your bridge is needed only to move thinking from one point to another but not to serve as a permanent span to carry two-way traffic. Sometimes we do a bridge in a few minutes. At other times, the bridge may take a week to set up and navigate and become an integral superstructure for new learning. The kind of bridge you choose should be consistent with the time and depth of the learning episode you are designing. Don't feel bound by rigid construction specifications or protocols.

Learning Circle Considerations

When you have an opportunity to talk with colleagues about their teaching, you can compare notes on the ways they surface prior knowledge and assess existing understanding in their students. Talk with others in your department or grade level about how they find out what students already know or think about a concept, process, or attitude as they begin a learning episode. Others teaching the same topic may use different language to talk about ways to engage students. Some may describe an advanced organizer, some an anticipatory set, and others may refer to a motivator. You can open their bag of tricks, look for ways to revisit familiar activities, and pick up tips for using them while keeping with the characteristics described above. For example, one of your colleagues uses the movie *Dead Poets Society* as a motivator for a unit on poetry or on teenage tendencies toward self-destruction. You might consider modifying this activity by just showing a video clip of the teacher encouraging students to tear pages out of their textbooks that describes rating poetry on a rather sterile matrix about style, and then use the clip as a springboard to a discussion about whether poetry needs passion or prescription to capture readers' attention.

In conversation with your colleagues, also explore what they know about poetry and how they learned it; this can help you prepare for a similar discussion with students. We are frequently surprised by the variety of things that teachers surface in this kind of brainstorming. They know about poetry from high school or college courses, from movie or television programs, from reading poetry by friends or partners, from going to poetry readings or slams, from attending fringe festivals or listening to public radio, and from trying to write and read their own poetry. Their experiences offer you a bridge to what your secondary students know about poetry and how they know it.

Another good focus question for a discussion with your colleagues is how your *situation* purpose or learning goal might help your students meet state or national standards. This conversation might give you information about what your students study before they are in your class and what they are expected to know for subsequent classes. The more you understand about what your students might already know or need to know, the better you can design your learning episodes to take advantage of expectations your teaching colleagues have at a federal, state, or local level. If you can give your colleagues feedback about what students really understand when you involve them in learning, then you are in a better position to influence the quality as well as the content of their learning.

Concluding Remarks

We understand that time devoted to setting up learning is limited by the pressures of school bells, unrelated content, textbook length, disciplinary programs, and other external factors that impinge on a careful setup of each learning episode. We have found, however, that the bridge is an investment in student engagement that pays handsome dividends in terms of student learning time. Time invested up front in the manner we've described will reduce time lost to disruption, low motivation, and discipline problems. We use the notion of building a bridge between prior knowledge and new learning as an active construction metaphor for this element of our learning design. You can provide the body of learning that students will gain access to and the points at which knowledge will be anchored, but each student must construct his or her own bridge between prior knowledge and new learning. Student bridges vary. We urge you to draw upon opening or introductory activities that have been successful for you in the past and modify them as necessary to accommodate our characteristics. Let students create their own bridge between prior knowledge and new learning.

Chapter

4

Asking Questions

Good questions acknowledge the possibilities of thought and are built around varying forms of thinking. Good questions are directed toward broad learning and evaluative thinking rather than toward what has been learned in a narrow sense.

—Norris Sanders, *Classroom Questions: What Kinds?*
(1966, p. ix)

This chapter describes the fourth element of our constructivist learning design (CLD) called *questions*. Like Sanders (1966), we believe that "good questions recognize the wide possibilities of thought." Perhaps the most compelling act of education is asking a question rather than answering one. An open-ended and well-timed question will prompt learners to seek an answer and set them off on a path to new knowledge. Usually, the best questions are those that learners ask themselves, those that prompt evaluative thinking. Socrates founded a tradition of teachers asking questions to help students clarify their thinking. The questions that teachers ask and the way that they ask them sustains or stifles learning for students. In the spirit of great questions, we describe this element of the learning design process. Few lesson-planning schemes ask teachers to consider what questions might instigate, inspire, or integrate student thinking during a learning episode. We encourage you to focus on clarifying student thinking by using careful questioning.

We position *questions* as the fourth element in the sequence. You have already imagined how the bridge and situation might unfold as students think about how they will accomplish the task presented to them. Thinking about questions prompts you to consider how students might think and how you can understand, clarify, and respond to their thinking. If you anticipate student confusion, misconceptions, and questions in advance, then you are better prepared to respond to them in a positive way that encourages real learning.

Characteristics of Questions

We conceive of questions as prompts or responses used by teachers to initiate, extend, or synthesize student thinking during a learning episode. Questions take place during each element of the learning design. You can think about specific questions that you can use to introduce the situation, arrange the groupings, set up the bridge, support active learning, prompt exhibits, and encourage reflections.

Questions fall into several categories. Engaging or *guiding questions,* related to setting up the situation or bridge, are thoughtfully crafted in advance. *Anticipated questions* from students can help you frame responses that encourage students to explain their thinking or that support them in continuing to think for themselves. Extending or *clarifying questions* are often responses to student requests for information or explanations as they work to accomplish the task presented in the situation. Expected or explaining or *integrating questions* are typically asked to provoke students to synthesize their thinking for an exhibit or for reflections as the learning episode is coming to closure.

Guiding questions should

- Create opportunities for student thinking

- Be broad enough to have multiple answers or several ways to produce an answer

- Engage or intrigue the students in the answer

Anticipated questions can

- Help you imagine how students will try to accomplish the task

- Surface notions that will confuse students while accomplishing the task

- Identify common student misconceptions

Clarifying questions should

- Build on anticipated questions

- Not imply the answers

- Sustain thinking by framing another question

- Show an understanding of student thinking and probe it

- Gently challenge misconceptions and extend thinking

Integrating questions should

- Surface what each student in a group understands about the collaborative thinking

- Move the students toward a synthesis of group thinking

- Serve as a dipstick or quick check on when to present group thinking

Guiding Questions

Guiding questions are generally asked at the beginning of a learning episode. For "Vending Machine," you can divide students into groupings by what their favorite soft drink is and have them describe their choice. In "Fairy Tales," you could surface prior knowledge in the bridge by asking students to recall their experiences with fairy tales. In "Drawing an Animal," you can frame the task for students to accomplish in the situation by asking them to imagine a new animal for Brown Bear to see.

Guiding questions should create opportunities for student think-ing. Guiding questions provoke students to think. Thinking happens when we have to figure something out for ourselves, often something we have never done before. How can we possibly solve a problem we've never encountered? We can remember previous strategies or similar sit-uations. We can talk to people about what they would do. We can brain-storm. We can make sure we understand the problem. How can we ac-complish a task with the people and knowledge in our group? We can find out what each person knows how to do. We can put our heads to-gether and talk about who might address different parts of the task. How will we create a metaphor, answer a question, make a decision, or set a goal? What resources do we have available? How much time do we have? What should the end product look like? All these questions be-come further opportunities for thinking. If we expect students to think critically about how to address a situation, then we need to offer them guiding questions—so they can figure things out for themselves—rather than present them with answers in advance. This process can be uncom-fortable at first. Most of us were schooled in a tradition in which an-swers were given, information was packaged, we were told in advance how to address a problem, and we were given detailed directions for ac-complishing a task. Most of us do, however, deal with challenges such as marriage, parenthood, work, and perhaps injury or illness, without benefit of teachers and textbook but with the encouragement of others. We learn to work through life's lessons with the support of our commu-nity, not by consulting an instruction manual.

Guiding questions should be broad enough to have multiple an-swers or several ways to produce an answer. It is important not to nar-row the expected answers to a single *correct* response. Narrow ques-tions don't encourage students to move beyond the recall of a fact, definition, or concept. Consequently, guiding questions should have several possible answers or suggest various ways for students to arrive at an answer. Guiding questions can even be a bit ambiguous so that an-swers are not immediately obvious. The situation of the fairy tales de-sign asks middle school students to describe their previous experience with fairy tales, to develop their own definitions of a fairy tale, and then to identify the common elements in fairy tales. A variety of different ex-periences surface when students analyze, compare, and define fairy tales and look for common elements. Questions prompt multiple responses yet are designed so students can work toward a definition and identify common elements.

Guiding questions should engage or intrigue students in the answer. The nature of the question asked can set the stage to engage students in learning or to turn them off. For example, "What is your favorite fairy tale and why?" produced a much less personal response from students than, "What is your previous experience with fairy tales?" The opportunity for students to make a connection to their memories seemed more intriguing to middle school students than debating the merits of different fairy tales. Most of them could tell stories about fairy tales from their own lives— such as how hearing about the troll in *The Three Billy Goats Gruff* made them hesitant to cross small bridges on hiking trails. Perhaps a good way to test a question to see if it engages students is to answer it yourself and see where your thinking goes. If you are not intrigued with your own imaginings, then students may not be either. Try out questions on teacher colleagues, your own children, or some students from another class to measure the question's potential for firing the imagination.

Anticipated Questions

Anticipated questions generally help us to see where there might be openings in a learning episode to explore or extend student thinking. We see these openings occurring when students surface conflicting or challenging ideas, seek an explanation from the teacher, offer prescriptive advice to one another, or express surprise at an idea or discussion. The first time you teach a learning episode, this kind of anticipation will be very important. Once you have seen a learning episode unfold, you should see clearly the utility of your learning design. You can make notes about what worked and how you would modify your approach the next time.

Anticipated questions help you imagine how students will try to accomplish the task. A good first step is to put yourself in the role of a student working with peers to accomplish the task. Thoroughly imagine what they would do. Don't be afraid to immerse yourself in imagining! Get comfortable in a chair, close your eyes, and visualize yourself as a student addressing the task with a group of peers. What would you talk about as you began to think together? What would you want to know about accomplishing the task? How would the completed task look? Who would do what in the group? How would you record your thinking while accomplishing the task? You might try doing the task yourself. You could find pitfalls or shortcuts that would help you frame responses to students when these same aspects appeared during the learning episode. This could also help you think about a way of framing a rubric with the students as a way of introducing assessment of the task. You might preview your task with a colleague, or with a student to get their reactions. All of this preparation should serve you well so you can anticipate student questions, provide support, and promote thinking.

Anticipated questions might surface potentially confusing aspects of the learning episode. Such questions help you anticipate later questions that students may ask. What parts of the task or your introduction of it could seem unclear to students? Where are the potential points of confusion? How could you help students clarify their understanding without giving them answers? What questions might help them sort out their confusion?

Anticipated questions might identify common student misconceptions. Such troubleshooting is particularly helpful for designing an appropriate bridge to review what the students currently know or think. As we anticipated questions in the "Moon View" design, we realized that students might attribute the phases of the moon to shadows of the earth. We framed the question, "What is an eclipse?" as a way of redirecting student thinking. Usually that did set them off in another direction, but if they were still unclear, then we would ask, "Do we have an eclipse of the moon most of the time?" A misconception that arose in the "Trading Partners" design was that many of our trading partners didn't trade with continents other than North America. Aware of this perspective, we designed a bridge that asked students to describe trade between continents other than North America.

Clarifying Questions

Clarifying questions are usually asked as students think together to accomplish the task. Clarifying questions are responses to requests for information, explanations, or confirmation about ideas from small groups or individuals. As you move among collaborative groups, don't just respond to such requests but probe what students were thinking that led to the request.

Clarifying questions should build on anticipated questions. The major reason for anticipating student questions is to prepare clarifying questions in response. If you don't anticipate questions, you may feel caught off guard or blindsided by questions from students. If that does happen, a good response is to have students explain why they asked the question or to describe the conversation that led to their question. This is not a ploy to buy time but rather is a facilitation of student learning. Very few good tasks have easy answers.

Clarifying questions should not imply answers. One of our most enduring images of teachers is that they had the answers to our questions. We are comforted by the idea that our students expect us to have valuable knowledge or to know something they don't. But if we just respond to their questions with the answers, without knowing why they asked the question, then we miss an opportunity to understand their thinking.

Clarifying questions should sustain thinking by framing another question. Our students often express their frustration at never receiving a specific answer from us when they ask a question. As we begin to work with a class, the first question from groups is often, "Do we have the right answer?" When we ask them how they might check or confirm their answers themselves, students who have always received rewards or validation from teachers feel cognitive dissonance as they grapple with their expectations. Highly successful students complain the most, whereas students who were often marginalized in traditional class-rooms begin to flourish.

Clarifying questions should show an understanding of student thinking and probe it. The best response seeks the root of student think-ing. The more you can probe students to elaborate on what they think and why they asked a question, the more likely they are to come to their own realization of what makes sense and what doesn't. In other words, they make their own meaning to construct their own knowledge.

Clarifying questions should gently challenge misconceptions and extend thinking. When students first told us that fairy tales derive from real-life experiences, we were surprised. We were tempted to correct them, but when we questioned them about their beliefs, they reported a family story or legend that had captured their imaginations as a child. To disrupt their misconception without damaging their credibility, we asked them why stories about Santa Claus or the tooth fairy are told to children. Sometimes a gentle challenge or disrupting question is most effective in letting students save face and reconsider existing beliefs that led to their thinking.

Integrating Questions

Integrating questions are typically asked as students have almost accomplished the task. Integrating questions are aimed at groups of students as they bring their working or thinking to a close. These ques-tions often arise during a quick pass around the class after the teacher has given a two-minute warning that the exhibit or presentation of stu-dent thinking is going to begin.

Integrating questions should surface what each student in a group understands about the collaborative thinking. As you move quickly from group to group, you might ask one of the students who has not been particularly vocal to explain what the group has been thinking. Even if each person is not going to present, you have a fast check on what some students understand.

Integrating questions should move the students toward a synthesis of group thinking. Sometimes group members have not agreed on a final answer and need to be urged to agree on what they will present. One approach is to ask about points of disagreement in their thinking and offer a few questions that could point them toward a resolution. You might be able to negotiate a compromise that will move them to an exhibit. Some groups negotiate a minority report to include everyone's thinking.

Integrating questions should serve as a dipstick or quick check on when to present group thinking. At times, the task students are asked to accomplish is more difficult for them than you anticipated. Moving from group to group, you may discover that none of them is making progress. You might be able to identify a point of confusion and have a short discussion with the whole group or give a hint that will move it forward. At other times, students will move toward closure much faster than you anticipated, and you will need to move them to an exhibit of their thinking sooner than anticipated. Often students claim to be ready to present their thinking, but as you ask them for a brief review, you find they obviously need more time to refine their presentation. We use questions such as, "Tell me the big idea in your thinking in 15 seconds," or "Can everyone explain the group's thinking?" If the answers are not positive, they may need more time to talk among themselves until all group members understand.

Examples of Questions Elements

In this section, we offer examples of questions in four CLDs taken from a dozen designs that are in the Resources section. These designs address four different levels of students. The primary (K-3) CLD is from fine arts and is about drawing animals. The intermediate (3-6) example is from science and is about moon view. The middle school (6-9) sample is from language arts and is about fairy tales. The high school (9-12) illustration is from social studies and is about trading partners. We chose examples from four subjects to emphasize the utility of the CLD. Review these four sample questions and note that each includes guiding, integrating, and clarifying questions based on anticipated questions from students. Then consider how each example aligns with our characteristics. Do guiding questions create opportunities for student thinking that engage students and have several possible answers? Do anticipated questions suggest how students might accomplish the task and expose potential confusions or misconceptions? Do clarifying questions build on imagined questions, raise other questions without giving answers, and challenge student thinking? Do integrating questions explore students' understanding of group thinking, move it toward a synthesis, and help students know when to present their ideas? Different questions will certainly be more appropriate at different times. Compare the following examples (see Figure 4.1) with these criteria and determine whether each of the questions satisfies our element characteristics. After considering these four examples, reexamine them in the context of the whole learning design.

Theory

Questioning is an art that requires thought and practice. Recently we found ourselves watching Bob Ross, a remarkable artist who creates his paintings on PBS and encourages people to put the images in their minds onto canvas. His perspective on painting is that the more you practice the better you paint. We feel the same way about asking questions—the more questions you ask, the better you become at questioning. He also reminds us that it takes practice to move images from your mind's eye to the canvas. Questions begin in our imagination and then move into the public sphere of the learning community.

Applying constructivist learning principles requires teachers to move away from asking students to recall specific answers to asking questions that encourage student thinking. This process is not as easy as it sounds. Most of us have spent at least two decades as students of teaching in elementary school, middle school, high school, and college. The model we experienced was teachers asking questions with specific answers. Students were expected to recall information from text readings, lecture notes, or lab assignments. Tests using true or false, multiple-choice, fill-in-the-blanks, or even short-answer formats sent a message to us that factual information was valued more than thoughtful analysis or explanation. Moving away from those models takes determination. Like our students, we suffer our own cognitive dissonance. Students seem to feel better if you give them the answer—this is an

FIGURE 4.1

Example Questions Elements

Questions 20 minutes	**Primary Grades: Fine Arts—Drawing Animals** The teacher reads *Brown Bear, Brown Bear, What Do You See?* again. This time, the teacher asks, "What other animal could we put here, and what color could it be?" Students are encouraged to be inventive and not criticize "polka-dot salamanders." Student: "Should I make my parrot green like the picture book or a new color?" Teacher: "Is your animal real or imagined? What sounds does your animal make? Where might your animal live?"
Questions 20 minutes	**Intermediate Grades: Science—Moon View** Groups are asked to draw a diagram of the relationship between the sun, the earth, and the phases of the moon. What are the phases of the moon? Isn't the curve on the moon just the result of the shadow of the earth? Why do we see the moon during the day? Do people on the other side of the earth see the moon in the same phase as we do? Why isn't the moon always in eclipse when the earth is between the moon and the sun? What is an eclipse of the sun? Where is the moon in the sky? How big is the moon compared to the earth? How far is the moon from the earth?
Questions 15 minutes	**Middle School: Language Arts—Fairy Tales** Students organize into groups and get paper, markers, and tape. They develop their definition of a fairy tale and list common characteristics of fairy tales. What were your previous experiences with fairy tales? How would you define a fairy tale? What are common characteristics of fairy tales? How do your definitions compare with the experts? Were your definitions and lists as precise? After seeing the other groups' and reading the experts' definitions and lists, what would you add to your own? Which definition was more meaningful to you and would be more helpful in writing your own fairy tale? Why are we studying fairy tales? Where did fairy tales come from? What are fairy tales from other cultures?
Questions 2 weeks	**High School: Social Studies—Trading Partners** Students select an occupation and evaluate its relationship to international trade. What are the roles and responsibilities of your occupation? What goods or services does your company produce or offer and how are they used in the local region? Nationally? Internationally? Is there a link between what you do and the products of any of the six continents we talked about? How will your occupation be affected by changes in international trade?

accepted response and someone knows it, so all they have to do is remember it. When students ask a question and you respond with a question that challenges or extends their thinking, they often object with, "Just tell us the answer!" or, "What do we learn when you answer our questions with a question?" It is harder for them to think about your question than to remember an answer. But how will they learn to think if they don't have an opportunity to practice thinking?

In the last century, there has been an explosion of information, and there will be much more information generated in the new millennium.

The focus of education must move away from memorizing to thinking—thinking about how we think, how we learn, and how we access information. Twenty years ago, a primary teacher colleague, Gail Gallagher, asked these questions: "When you are in conversation, how do you know what you are going to say next? How do we know kids are learning to read before they can read? Why do we expect all kids to read in first grade?" These kinds of questions can provoke profound thinking for the askers and for those who engage with them in trying to find answers. Often these questions produce not conclusive answers but rather wonderful new questions that provoke more thinking. If our focus in teaching is on questions rather than answers, then our students should be encouraged to think, to ask, and to answer their own questions. We believe questions, which are the basis for constructivist learning principles, begin the process of making meaning for ourselves and are the foundation for education in a democracy.

Different types of questions emerge from different contexts of learning. The concept of *openings* is adapted from an analysis of facilitation sessions for DMI (developing mathematical ideas) by Geist and Remillard (1998). They studied elementary teachers engaged in a professional development experience centered on materials for DMI. Their observations and interviews with facilitators led them to four major categories of openings in the curriculum during which facilitators needed to gently nudge participants and redirect them toward thinking about the math concepts under consideration rather than deciding on a *final answer*. In all learning episodes, questions are the levers that move students from current understanding to making meaning in new ways.

Precedents

There is precedence for our questions element in Benjamin Bloom's taxonomy of educational objectives in the cognitive domain, Norris Sanders' kinds of classroom questions, Ned Flanders' description of questioning strategies, and James Gallagher's observation of four categories of questions. All were addressing hierarchies of questions that progressed from basic memory or recall to higher level thinking. Each precedent is worth examining more closely.

In 1956, Benjamin Bloom headed a group of educational psychologists who developed a classification of levels of intellectual behavior important in learning. This became a taxonomy that included three overlapping domains: cognitive, psychomotor, and affective. Bloom and his colleagues encouraged teachers to move beyond simple recall questions toward questions in a hierarchy of six levels: knowledge, comprehension, application, analysis, synthesis, and evaluation. This work was significant and is often taught in teacher education programs, but the reality of classroom teaching rarely leads to questions that support higher-order thinking by students. One of our concerns about this conception of knowledge is that the first level is considered knowledge rather than mere information. We are not sure that students make much meaning or construct much knowledge if they only memorize and recall information.

We are reminded that the nature of the question affects the quality of thought required for the response. A question prompting only simple recall will not require much higher-order thinking or even encourage much thought at all on the part of students. Bloom's hierarchy can be used to frame situation tasks for students to accomplish that require higher levels of thinking. Some examples of verbs that represent thinking on each level are offered here.

1. *Knowledge:* arrange, define, duplicate, label, list, memorize, name, order, recognize, relate, recall, repeat, reproduce, or state

2. *Comprehension:* classify, describe, discuss, explain, express, identify, indicate, locate, recognize, report, restate, review, select, or translate

3. *Application:* apply, demonstrate, dramatize, employ, illustrate, interpret, operate, practice, schedule, sketch, solve, transcribe, use, or write

4. *Analysis:* analyze, calculate, categorize, compare, contrast, correlate, criticize, diagram, differentiate, discriminate, distinguish, examine, experiment, prove, question, or test

5. *Synthesis:* arrange, assemble, collect, compose, construct, create, design, develop, formulate, integrate, manage, organize, plan, prepare, propose, or set up

6. *Evaluation:* appraise, argue, assess, attach, choose, defend, estimate, evaluate, judge, predict, rate, select, support, or value

Teachers can often use these verbs in framing their guiding, clarifying, or integrating questions.

Flanders's (1966) descriptions of levels of classroom questions is similar to Bloom's hierarchy, but he elaborates on the lower levels and puts more emphasis on problem solving in the higher levels. He describes how teachers could use different kinds of questions in their classrooms to get students thinking at higher levels. The following summary represents a loose transcription of his kinds of categories.

1. Memory (recalling or recognizing information)

2. Translation (deciphering symbols or technical language)

3. Interpretation (discovering relationships between definitions, facts, generalizations, theories, or values)

4. Application (addressing life-like problems and identifying approaches for solving them)

5. Analysis (breaking a problem into solvable bits with conscious use of strategies)

6. Synthesis (solving problems by thinking creatively)

7. Evaluation (judging according to standards)

In an effort to promote higher levels of student thinking, Flanders (1970) helped teachers move from writing objectives to crafting questions. Teaching should be a process of discovery. As a teacher, you can assist this process by asking clarifying and penetrating questions that require students to go beyond superficial responses.

There are numerous taxonomies for classifying questions. The categories listed below are based on the work of James Gallagher et al. (1970), who define four categories of questions—cognitive memory, convergent, divergent, and evaluative.

1. Cognitive memory questions require the student to reproduce facts or other content through the use of such processes as recognition, rote memory, and selective recall. An example of a cognitive memory question is, *Can you tell me when Christopher Columbus first landed in the Americas?*

2. Convergent questions require the student to generate new information that leads to the correct or conventionally accepted answer. Given or known information usually determines the correct response. An example of a convergent question is, *Could you summarize for us the author's major point?*

3. Divergent questions require the student to generate his or her own data independently in a data-poor situation, or to take a new perspective on a given topic. Divergent questions have no right answer. An example of a divergent question is, *How might the history of the United States have been different if the pilgrims had landed on the West Coast instead of on the East Coast?*

4. Evaluative questions require the student to make value judgments and decisions regarding the goodness, correctness, or adequacy of information, based on a criteria usually set by the students. An example of an evaluative question is, *How has the history of North American colonization and genocide of Native peoples been portrayed by 20th-century historians?* This question requires the students to revisit how they were taught history and from whose perspective history is presented and to judge the portrayal of historical events for themselves.

Although the precedents we cite in this section are more than 30 years old, landmark research by John Goodlad (1984) and others indicates that little has changed in classrooms. Most teacher questions still solicit recall and recognition responses from students. We encourage you to think carefully about the questions you will ask as you design a learning episode and prepare for anticipated questions from students. Preparing to ask questions is the serious work of teaching and must be considered in advance. Although experienced teachers appear to wing it with wonderful questions, they have years of experience with students in similar learning episodes. New teachers can benefit from as much forethought about questions as possible.

Teachniques for Questions

Asking the Right Questions

Questions are a key to learning! Your questions set the tone for engaging the students in their own thinking and learning. These questions guide your thinking and adjustments as learning unfolds. As you anticipate student questions you can respond in a way that doesn't merely give an answer but that encourages students to keep thinking about the situation. A colleague of ours reports that Japanese teachers have thick plan books for individual lessons they have developed in teams. Much of each book is devoted to anticipated student questions and explanations, so teachers are prepared to respond positively and to support students in thinking through their constructs.

It Feels Good to Give Answers

Most of us really enjoy knowing something and being able to share it with another person who asks a question or seeks our advice. We are affirmed as valuable people when we can give an answer that satisfies another person. The principles of constructivist learning require teachers to take a different role, to find out why students are asking the questions, and to encourage them to clarify their thinking. Ask them why they are asking the question and what they already know. Try to get inside the mind of the questioners and find out where they are in their thinking; then ask a question to get them moving along in their learning. It can be hard to relearn or reconstruct our concept of teacher and replace the role of question-answerer with the role of thinking-questioner. Such a change is essential if we are to support learners in constructing their own knowledge.

Sometimes a Small Change Causes Big Confusion

In a math methods class with prospective teachers, we used a familiar situation. Usually we present a can of tennis balls and ask students to decide whether it is taller or farther around and then to explain their answer. One morning, the tennis balls were not available, so we grabbed three oranges and asked the students to imagine a cylindrical container that would hold those oranges tightly. With one class we used the tennis ball analogy in setting up the situation, but in the next class we didn't. The second class took as their task deciding whether the container for the oranges needed to have more room at the top or around the sides to accommodate the oranges. This led to several surprising questions, and we figured out that by substituting new objects, we had produced unanticipated confusion. We hadn't thought through the last-minute substitution very carefully.

Two-Minute Warnings

Trying to bring group thinking about a task to a close can be tricky. Some students are not ready, others are ready and waiting, and still others would benefit from rethinking. But to have enough time for students to share their thinking, we usually take the temperature of the working groups by announcing a two-minute warning when most seem ready to present. Those who have finished can be encouraged to extend their thinking or refine their presentation. Those not ready or in need of rethinking can learn from the other exhibits of thinking. Two minutes is just about enough time to let the groups finish their conversations or decide what to postpone until later and what to present.

Learning Circle Considerations

Determining the nature of effective questions that can elicit or extend student thinking is an excellent topic for discussion with your learning circle. Japanese teachers of mathematics often work together to develop lessons, and they follow a format that is very similar to our CLD. Some of their work can be seen on the videos accompanying the Third International Math and Science Study (TIMSS) (National Center for Education

Statistics, 1998). Their lessons are often created by a group of teachers who meet while two colleagues are teaching half of three classes, freeing one teacher (from every group of three classes) for planning. After planning for several months, one teacher teaches the lesson while the others observe and make notes. Then they meet together to analyze the lesson. They develop thick binders about the lesson, complete with anticipated student questions and typical results of student work. You might take a learning design you are developing to your grade-level team or learning-circle colleagues and seek their advice about student questions that you have anticipated and other questions that you have considered for the learning episode. As they review what you expect, their feedback will strengthen your learning design.

Concluding Remarks

Recent research suggests that teachers ask between 300 and 400 questions daily. However, not much has changed since classroom observations in 1912. Most of these questions encourage recall of facts or information previously given by the teacher and ingested by the students. We urge you to think carefully about the questions you ask students. As you move through a learning episode, the nature of questions changes from guiding student thinking to clarifying their thinking to integrating their thinking. These kinds of questions are not focused on answers but on making the process of student thinking more visible for individuals, small groups, and the larger community. This approach is intended to support student learning by clarifying their thinking as they make their own meaning and construct knowledge together.

Chapter 5

Arranging Exhibits

Human beings are by nature social, interactive learners. We observe how others do it and see if it works for us. We learn to drive and cook this way. And we learn how to handle ideas this way. We check out our ideas, argue with authors, bounce issues back and forth, ask friends to read our early drafts, talk together after we've seen a movie, pass on books we've loved. We attend meetings, argue things out, share stories, and gossip. In these ways, we extend our understanding of others and ourselves.

—Deborah Meier, *The Power of Their Ideas: Lessons for America From a Small School in Harlem* (1995, p. 153)

This chapter describes the fifth element of our constructivist learning design, which we call the *exhibit*. The term "exhibit" may conjure up a gallery, a museum, an artist's portfolio, an architect's studio, or any collection of completed products on display. We use the notion of an exhibit to describe student presentation of the artifacts they created to accomplish a task framed by the *situation*. Requiring students to show work is common in education, but this is usually done in private by turning in assignments to the teacher for grading. As this process moves from individual, private acts to more open and public exhibits, the power of social interaction shapes learning profoundly. We react to the ideas, questions, and observations of others viscerally as well as intellectually. The basic social skills of critical thinking, communicating, and relating are required for an effective public presentation. When the results of a learning process are private and hidden, then others can't engage in and learn from these fundamental social processes of framing and defending a point of view.

Characteristics of an Exhibit

In this exhibit element, our focus is on groups of students making a public presentation of the artifacts they have generated to document their accomplishment of a task during a learning episode. As students have an opportunity to show what they know to others, they take their accomplishment of tasks and the documentation of their learning more seriously. The product of their own thinking becomes a basis for their presentations and provides an opportunity for peers to review their work. We see students listen more attentively to one another and support one another in explaining their thinking when they present their work to peers. They also engage in more authentic work when they are preparing an explanation of their thinking for one another. This public presentation also provides a time and place for students to respond to questions from the teacher or their peers about their artifacts or thinking. The teacher can use student presentations of artifacts to decide what has been learned, to design future learning episodes, and to guide the whole class and the individual students in a consideration of the learning episode. Teachers can also ask students to make explanations of their thinking that respond to state or national standards.

The characteristics of an exhibit are these:

- Students generate artifacts to document their accomplishment of a task.

- Students present their artifacts publicly and explain their thinking.

- Students respond to questions from their teacher or peers.

- Teachers determine what learning has taken place.

■ Teachers guide student considerations of the learning episode.

■ Teachers align student explanations of thinking with requirements of state or national standards.

Students generate artifacts to document their accomplishment of a task. Artifacts are as varied as the terrain traveled during the learning episode. Some examples include writing a description on cards and giving a verbal presentation; making a graph, chart, or other visual representation; acting out or role playing their impressions; constructing a physical representation with models; and making videotapes, photographs, or audiotapes to display accomplishment of a task. In addition, a paper or electronic portfolio is a fairly comprehensive exhibit used by many teachers within or across content areas.

Artifacts must reflect the task and address the goals of both learner and evaluator. One artifact that suggests understanding of a concept is a visual metaphor. For example, juniors and seniors in a high school career course might draw a picture of what tools they will use in certain professions. Some will sketch a toolbox and talk about carpentry tools, some will draw a computer keyboard or monitor as they think about technical careers, and still others will sketch a stethoscope and talk about their hope of studying medicine.

If the task to be accomplished is more step-by-step and requires analysis or problem solving, a Venn diagram might be a useful artifact for learner and evaluator. Two middle school science teachers asked students to sort a list of animals by type: pets, domesticated, and wild. They found a pig in all three categories. After reviewing their diagram for the class, students had to explain why some animals fit only one category whereas others appear in the intersection of one or more circles.

An artifact can capture understanding about a concept or idea from the most simple or early stages of thinking to later complex stages. For example, high school social studies teachers can ask each student to write a sentence or paragraph about the colonizing of our country. Such an open-ended assignment will generate a tremendous breadth of feedback for teachers. They can assess the "so what" that each student carried from previous study; identify the source of information from a textbook, miniseries, or visit to Colonial Williamsburg; judge the sophistication of knowledge; and even gauge the student's expository writing ability. The teacher can also ask students where they got their ideas before they write or wait and discern that information after gathering the responses.

Students present their artifacts publicly and explain their thinking. After most groups have accomplished the task framed by the *situation,* we ask students to present the artifacts they generated and to explain their thinking. This public explanation of their thinking is the key to our construct of an *exhibit.* Students realize they are expected to think, produce artifacts that document their accomplishment of tasks, present these artifacts publicly, and explain their thinking. Learning takes on an immediate urgency, social character, and personal relevance not often anticipated or appreciated by students who are not engaged in learning or invested in making meaning when they just sit and listen to a teacher.

Students respond to questions from their teacher or peers. As each question is presented, the exhibitor is challenged to retell the story of accomplishing the task, articulate reasons certain things were done, and look for ways to help the questioner make sense of the exhibit. This responsibility moves the learner quickly into the role of a presenter who is active rather than of a listener who is passive. Teachers have the opportunity to ask probing questions, modify questions to reflect the sophistication of the learner, and individualize the framework of inquiry.

Teachers determine what learning has taken place. The task of evaluation is much more straightforward when multiple measures are available. Skillful teachers assess student learning informally, intuitively, and without benefit of documentation every day. They use invisible assessments to make myriad decisions—when or whether one student or many students have mastered a concept or process, which parts of a complex curriculum might be focused on or abandoned, and what kinds of lessons have been most effective in supporting new learning. Teachers can make their thinking more visible to students by showing how student artifacts and reflections influence the next learning episodes.

Students need to develop skills of self-evaluation. Because little time is available to unpack or reflect on teacher or student observations, students may not be aware of what evaluation has occurred and may not gain independent capabilities of self-assessment or peer assessment. But when students present the tasks they have accomplished, they are forced to move into the realm of analysis and interpretation.

It is essential that teachers act as anthropologists, keeping records of student work. If teachers and students don't have a paper or electronic trail to show gradual or rapid growth in student learning, both students and teachers are at the mercy of a single measurement, such as a one-time standardized exam, to show what they *don't* know. Parents, who are important stakeholders in student assessment, can become powerful advocates for appropriate assessment if they are introduced to high-quality documentation of their child's learning. For all these reasons, we advocate making visible both existing and new learning.

Teachers guide student considerations of the learning episode. In almost every learning episode, students can make a record of their current and new understanding. These artifacts are made by individuals demonstrating existing knowledge about a concept (know, want to know, learned—KWL), by learning circles working cooperatively to complete a task, or by a larger group or class. A student exhibit can be structured to provide teachers and other students with both individual and group assessments. For instance, in our "Spanish Song" CLD, each student translates the same song but is encouraged to think independently about interpretation of the lyrics. Teachers and students are reassured that each student is doing a common exercise of translation and an individual exercise of interpretation.

In another example, students study the civil rights movement. As a bridge, students jot down their key understandings and sources of information about the civil rights movement. The teacher can then group them by topic interest, by source of information, or randomly so that they can compare responses and generate an artifact that shows their combined understanding of the topic. For instance, each group could brainstorm about key activists in the civil rights movement and present their list to the class. Then new groups could be formed to study each activist. As part of their documentation, groups could make a placard that each activist might have carried. This exhibit is specific to the teacher's purpose—that students understand the importance of individuals to this particular movement. Finally, the teacher can set about revisiting the social, historical, and economic context for students and add new information in a strategic way.

Teachers align student explanations of thinking with requirements of state or national standards. Teachers often are ambivalent as they seek to broaden their classroom-assessment practices in an educational system that is increasingly pressured by external, standardized testing. As you become familiar with the formal assessment frameworks that your students face, you can incorporate realistic examples into your classroom assessment practices. For instance, our state has some comprehensive problem-solving assessments for middle school math. These assessments are appropriate and useful in daily math teaching.

Efforts to improve technological literacy can be combined with a social studies curriculum. Groups or individuals can create a Web site or a hyperstudio presentation about Native Americans as key stakeholders in American history who are often overlooked. Students can conduct research to learn about the contemporary treaty rights of tribes in their region. In states such as Washington and Minnesota, they can document how fishing treaty rights currently affect their communities. Students can create a public relations Web site to educate all members of the community. Technology has few standardized assessments, and recently developed international standards. Therefore, students can work with the teacher to decide how the Web site will be evaluated for both social studies and technology and to set standards of quality that projects must meet. When students are invited to help construct the evaluation framework, teachers and students can refine the assignment and expand their vision about learning from merely completing a high school assignment to learning something that will be useful for a lifetime.

In all three cases described above (in connection with social studies, Spanish, and technology), regional or national standards can be used to frame the choice of content and the type of evaluation used. Assessment of student learning in relation to standards can be done with teacher-generated rubrics or, more effectively, with a rubric designed jointly by students and teachers. Teachers can then encourage students to design their exhibits to meet existing standards rather than following standard instructions. The work of Ted Sizer (1992) and the Coalition of Essential Schools offers standards-based exhibitions linked directly to external standards. Deborah Meier (1995) suggests that standards emerge from collaborative decision making by students, teachers, parents, and community members about what kinds of displays can best demonstrate student learning.

The term *accountability* is in vogue as educators, parents, and other consumers of the products of schooling seek ways to assess the qualifications of recent graduates. From standardized testing to the more subjective portfolio, college admissions committees as well as employers want evidence of what young adults can do. Despite the overemphasis on standardized test scores, candidates for college or for employment are required to present credentials that cover a broad spectrum. As they move into future roles and responsibilities, students can carry with them exhibits they helped construct. Professionals making admissions and hiring decisions will get not only a clear view of what students know but also a glimpse into how they made sense of what they learned.

Examples of Exhibit Elements

In this section, we offer examples of an exhibit in four CLDs taken from a dozen designs that are in the Resources section. These designs address four different levels of students. The primary (K-3) CLD is from physical education and is about imitating animals. The intermediate (3-6) example is from media technology and is about Logo. The middle school (6-9) sample is from math and is about base blocks. The high school (9-12) illustration is from foreign language and is about Spanish songs. We chose examples from four subjects to emphasize the utility of the CLD. Review these four example exhibit elements and note that each includes students generating artifacts and students presenting their thinking. Then consider how each example aligns with our characteristics. Do these presentations and student responses to questions assist teachers in assessing student learning, in guiding class considerations of learning, and in aligning student explanations of thinking with standards? Compare the following examples (see Figure 5.1) with these criteria and decide whether different exhibit elements satisfy our characteristics. After comparing the four examples, you might want to review them in the context of the complete designs.

FIGURE 5.1

Example Exhibit Elements

Exhibit *24 minutes*	**Primary Grades: Physical Education—Imitating Animals** In the order of the new book, first the individuals and then the whole class acts out the movements of each animal after it sees another animal looking at it.
Exhibit *20 minutes*	**Intermediate Grades: Media Technology—Logo** When most students are done trying to make the largest equilateral triangle, they show to the class the triangle they made and the program to draw it. Later, students show to the class the circle they made and the program to draw it.
Exhibit *10-15 minutes per question*	**Middle School: Mathematics—Base Blocks** After each group has an opportunity to work out how to represent the problem, a solution, and the relationship between the two, the groups have a "see what we made parade," so each group can show its model to others and explain its work.
Exhibit *2 days*	**High School: Foreign Language—Spanish Songs** Groups sing their transcribed song in English. In Spanish, they present their findings about how Hispanic musical styles have influenced mainstream American music.

Theory

As we have discussed throughout this chapter, exhibits of learning are prominent in real life and in many parts of the elective curriculum. In real life, workers at all levels must demonstrate their abilities to do the job—whether punching picture buttons on the cash register at McDonald's or carrying a portfolio of graphic art to a potential employer on Madison Avenue. In fine arts, industrial arts, home economics, personal finance, journalism, athletics, and many other areas, the proof is in the pudding. Can the band play in tune, can the mechanic fix the small engine, can the business student balance a spreadsheet, can the philosophy student write a coherent argument, and can the athlete win a competition? The answers are exhibits in the real world. Exhibits are already evident in many courses in the comprehensive high school curriculum, too. Moreover, exhibits that capture a greater breadth of learning can be put in place in all the disciplines that are generally dependent on a few assessment strategies, disciplines such as science, math, social studies, and language arts or English.

Judging an exhibit requires courage. Many teachers rely on grading schemes with easily measured factors, such as attendance, tardiness, homework completion, and quizzes. To work primarily with a student's real product requires two things—the product and the knowledge to judge it. English teachers are notorious for marking grammatical errors—but they can also acknowledge the young writer who tells a compelling story. They must trust their own intuition about the potential of a young person to make a contribution to the literary world through prose or to the technological world by writing useful manuals. This step requires the courage of one's convictions in a system that rewards using neatly scored and normed tests to determine grades. Parents and other teachers also put pressure on teachers to measure small things and avoid the challenge of fostering and judging fully developed products. However, the quality of thinking presented at science fairs, debate meets, and journalism competitions is strong evidence in the case for students displaying their own work for others to examine. The same sense of production, display, and accomplishment takes place during the presentation of student portfolios during parent-teacher conferences at the end of a school term.

Precedents

The work of Theodore Sizer (1992) and the Coalition for Essential Schools includes exhibitions as part of the learning process. "This exhibition allows a student to demonstrate not only qualities of mind but also of persistence, habits of organization, and the ability to apply 'classroom knowledge' well beyond the confines of the school" (p. 80). His approach gained national prominence because of the work of the Coalition and of others such as Deborah Meier at Central Park East School. Completing the "Passages" of the Jefferson County Open School in Colorado and the "Validations" of the St. Paul Open School in Minnesota has been required of graduates for 30 years. These forms of authentic assessment are now advocated by a variety of sources including Grant Wiggins (1998). Documentation from Brenda Engel (1994), portfolios from Patricia Carini (1986), and alternative assessment from the North Dakota Study Group on Evaluation convened by Vito Perrone

(1991a) encouraged teachers to move from testing memorization of information to demonstrating student learning.

In the last decade, the portfolio has been the focus of authentic and appropriate assessment, but all portfolios are not alike. Mary Deitz (1995) describes several kinds of portfolios for different uses, including the presentation portfolio (résumé or album), the working portfolio (evidence that fulfills prescribed competencies, standards, or outcomes), and the learner portfolio (an envelope of the mind) (pp. 40-41). These three different displays offer students and teachers important ways to capture and portray their new learning. The presentation portfolio is the one most people think of as they imagine a photographer carrying her best offerings to a magazine editor or an eight-year-old third grader proudly showing an oft-edited and cleaned up essay. The working portfolio contains exhibits in the traditions of the Coalition of Essential Schools, which are designed to show that students have met a standard of achievement. Finally, the learner portfolio captures formative assessment by learner and teacher, offering to both new insights into the learner's emerging knowledge about a topic.

One learning episode can use the portfolio for different kinds of assessment. In the fairy tale example, a portfolio could contain the final student-authored fairy tale, versions of the same story from its inception, and student reflections about the evolving work. Convincing students to keep drafts for public review, however, is not easy—the first time we asked adult students to include their "sloppy copy" of an essay, the class exploded. Many individuals were very uncomfortable allowing others' gaze to fall on their most intimate struggles as writers. Young authors feel the same way. Teachers will need to create a culture that supports the exposure of early efforts, making those efforts a part of the work that is valued.

Teachniques for Exhibits

Recording and Reporting Thinking

During their thinking about a group explanation, students should keep individual records of their work to exhibit for peers. A skill that can be taught, good note taking or recording requires from students both discipline and determination. Teachers and students can model a variety of ways to keep notes, and teachers should wander around the classroom to ensure that all students are meeting a minimum standard of documentation. Again, it is critical that the information being recorded have some intrinsic value or it will be reduced to an exercise. We ask all students—not just a designated recorder—to make a record of the group's thinking. When the time comes to display their thinking during an exhibit, we ask students to choose their reporter randomly—for example, to select the oldest or youngest member of the group or the one whose birthday is closest to the day of the exhibit or the tallest or shortest student or the one who lives closest to or farthest from the school. Sometimes we ask specific individuals to report because of the unique or complex character of their thinking as we observed it in their group. We refer to this approach as *individual recording and selective reporting.*

Using the Record of Thinking

Students should be encouraged to learn and to use basic note taking processes that we call *recording*. For this process to be compelling, the students and the teacher must make use of the notes. For instance, if the group recorder writes down a list of ideas from a brainstorming session, the list should be transcribed and made public for the rest of the group and for the entire class. The items on the list should then be used in subsequent activities. In a recent class, we asked students to determine the characteristics of a good collaborator. Each student wrote down 5 characteristics; then each group recorder collected 10 of these; and finally, each group placed its list on the classroom whiteboard. These characteristics were discussed and typed into a long list, then e-mailed to the entire class. Each student will be drafting individual plans to improve her or his social skills as collaborators, and each will be encouraged to make use of the list the class initially created. The same characteristics that the students listed also appear in the textbook, but the level of ownership among students is greater with this strategy. Artifacts in this example include individual note cards or notebook entries, the recorder's notes, and the full group white board lists and e-mail message.

Teaching to Learn

Moving from personal note taking or recording to a public display of learning is a critical step in constructivist learning and teaching. Although concern that individual students must be held accountable might seem the most important reason for this transition, there are additional reasons. For example, "To teach is to learn twice over" is an adage that applies here. Jotting down a few notes does not require the same depth of understanding as does explaining a concept to others. When we present publicly, we prepare more carefully, we anticipate debate, and we learn that everyone does not make the same meaning of the concept that we do. Therefore, students must be prepared to explain and defend their thinking.

Keeping a Positive Tone

Positive group interactions are dependent on the exchange of valuable information. Constructivist learning cannot take place in an atmosphere of competition and bell curves, where speed counts and only one kind of learning style is valued. A variety of exhibits honors a variety of thinking styles and points of view. Brainstorming and presenting ideas both involve a great deal of trust and respect among students. A classroom climate of mutual respect and trust must be nurtured by the teacher so that students accept these values.

Valuing and Encouraging Divergent Thinking

School can be a place where imitation is a religion and divergence is ridiculed. Teachers and other adult role models must encourage and reward individuality and reject the idea that similarity means rigor. Similarity in exhibits might seduce teachers and students into thinking they are meeting a standard. But students benefit most from a diversity of presentations and ideas. Each student can keep a record of the group's explanation. Then one student or several students can be involved in reporting this explanation to other groups. Moreover, teachers can introduce students to many ways of producing artifacts that document new learning, then invite students to offer their own ideas. Several different ways of explaining the same *situation* may emerge from one class as each group finds its own approach. One task, for instance, may involve each group creating a pie chart for ease of comparison, whereas another task may require them to design a chart appropriate to their interpretation of data.

Identifying Exhibits in the Real World

Young people are the ultimate consumers of everything from media to fast food. Rather than decrying this reality, we might look to expensively funded commercial exhibits and borrow ideas from Madison Avenue. For instance, students can report on images from MTV, advertising campaigns, newspaper articles using graphs and charts, and Web site captions. They can evaluate the effectiveness of advertising messages and explore possibilities for borrowing from that field.

Learning Circle Considerations

There is no limit to the ways teachers can ask students to exhibit their thinking. In addition to students, other teachers are a vital source of novel learning displays—for several reasons. They are often teaching within the same curricular framework that you are. They have access to the same materials and budgets and are working within the same assessment frameworks, such as portfolios and standardized tests. We can stretch our notions of ways to demonstrate knowledge by looking outside of our schools and districts to observe the documentation strategies used by others. Signs in the supermarket, presentation materials used by an insurance or financial agent, new and used car sales materials, signage at the zoo, or labels in a historical exhibit all exemplify ways to exhibit ideas.

Teachers can work with colleagues and central office personnel to figure out ways to link district assessment efforts to CLD and to appropriate demonstrations of learning. With the tremendous emphasis on test scores, teachers need to meet increasing challenges in formative evaluation, with the intermediate evaluation or dipstick efforts that reflect student learning throughout the unit or the year. A proactive rather than reactive response to external assessment structures allows teachers to blend useful methods in satisfying themselves about what and how students are learning. A substantive, continuous assessment cycle will also give students and teachers more confidence as they approach summative assessments that are teacher generated and external measures such as standardized tests.

We worked with an art teacher who had her students set up an art show and act as critics for their own and others' work. Using the Discipline-Based Art Education or DBAE framework, students learned about the elements of artistic works; created their own drawings, paintings, or sculptures; and then examined one another's work in the light of the critical knowledge they had gained. At the end of the unit, parents and community members were invited to an exhibit of the children's work. Student grades were linked directly to their work as critics as well as to their art products.

Concluding Remarks

The high-quality exhibit has remained the province of teachers of fine arts, industrial technology, and now, computer-based coursework, while other teachers cling tenaciously to research papers and standardized tests. These latter tools must assume a place beside the many other assessment procedures available to us. When imagining our students taking their knowledge as writers, historians, and scientists into the real world, we know from our own experiences and from what the greater community tells us that they will be required to "show what they know." We are doing our students and ourselves a big favor if we enter into the spirit of showing what we know in our daily, weekly, monthly, or end-of-term practice of evaluation and assessments. This kind of performance assessment, linked to explanations of thinking, is becoming popular in state tests to determine if graduation benchmarks or grade-level learning requirements are being met.

Chapter

6

Inviting
Reflections

In a good design process, the conversation with the situation is reflective. In answer to the situation's back talk, designers reflect on the construction of the problem and on the strategies of the action or model that are implicit in their design.

—Donald Schøn, *The Reflective Practitioner* (1983, p. 79)

This chapter describes the sixth element of our CLD, which we call *reflections*. This final, critical element offers both learners and teachers the opportunity to think again about their individual and collective learning, to begin the integration of new learning with existing knowledge, to plan for application of new knowledge, and in many cases, to design strategies for the next learning episode. As Schøn (1983) suggests, through reflection, the designer or creator *converses* with the situation. When students are active designers of their own learning, their knowledge flows backward and forward in time. This knowledge must be situated in a continuum of learning episodes. Reflection is a process for integrating new knowledge.

Although many tangible ways to guide, enhance, and document reflection exist, this linkage between learning episodes is often overlooked or given short shrift in the everyday hustle and bustle of a classroom. We hope to make explicit the importance of this element in the learning and teaching process and offer many ways to structure *reflections*.

Characteristics of Reflections

Reflections is the last element in our CLD, although reflections occur throughout the entire learning episode. Reflections capture what students were actually thinking and learning, not what material was presented or covered. Reflections have two parts. In the first part, the teacher engages the full group in interpreting and making sense of what has happened. Teachers review the learning episode with students to determine what concepts, processes, and attitudes students will take away with them. A primary purpose for this review is to give teachers a chance to perceive student understandings that emerged during the learning episode. This process will assist teachers in evaluating the purpose, flow, and effectiveness of their learning design. Another purpose of teacher-led reflections is to allow teachers to revisit or restate concepts or understandings that were presented in limited or inappropriate ways by the teacher or by student groups. For example, a group of students may inadvertently give factual misinformation or perpetuate racial or gender stereotypes. Teachers have the challenge and the responsibility of reframing the new information in a way that saves face for the presenters but leads the students along a more appropriate path. Finally, teachers take time to link student learning to big ideas or standards set by the district, state, or involved professional organization.

In the second part, students reflect on what they thought about while accomplishing the task and seeing the *exhibit* of presentations by other groups. Reflections include what students remember thinking, feeling, imagining, and processing through internal dialogue. Students might also reflect on what they learned today that they won't forget tomorrow or on what they knew before, what they wanted to know, and what they actually learned.

What will the students do with their newfound knowledge? According to Schøn, the students have a conversation with the *situation*. Conversations are captured in print so students have a record of their learning and can self-assess. These records are used to compare knowledge from before and after the learning episode. They create a sense of accountability for both students and teacher. When students take time to document their reflection in a systematic way, accountability and assessment are built into the episode and the unit.

The characteristics of reflections are these:

- Teachers lead a collective consideration of the learning episode.

- Teachers gather data about individual student's understanding.

- Teachers connect the learning episode to big ideas and address common misconceptions.

- Students individually consider their thinking during the learning episode.

- Students record their thinking to document learning.

- Students revisit their thinking after the learning episode.

Teacher-led reflections can occur in a variety of ways including class conversations, collective processing, group dialogues, or individual writing that is shared with the group. It is important for teachers to be strategic and equitable about gathering student feedback during the full-group activity. In this collective reflection, teachers and students consider what has gone on in the exhibit section of the CLD. For students, these considerations offer a supportive framework for thinking collectively and drawing meaning from the learning episode. This is especially important for students whose ideas are less popular. The teacher must show respect for them and their ideas so that other students learn to respond in the same way.

This most critical aspect of learning is often missed because of the nature of classroom teaching. Many of us teach to the bell and don't feel we can afford time to just reflect. This behavior is also driven by classroom management traditions that encourage teachers to keep students busy until the end of class so they don't become unruly. This habit must be changed for reflective activities to take place on a regular basis. Be assured that well-designed reflections are compelling and will keep students' attention well focused. Conducted thoughtfully, they are a more productive way to manage classroom time and keep students engaged at the end of a class session.

Teachers lead a collective consideration of the learning episode. The first part of this element involves teachers using the information about student learning that they have gleaned from the exhibit to lead a class conversation about the learning episode. This might play itself out as a class discussion of the different artifacts and explanations of thinking presented by groups, as a debriefing of groups by asking them to compare their work with others', or by asking groups to decide about holding or abandoning their perspective. Many different ways exist to consider a learning episode with a class. These include discussing what they learned, asking them how they might approach a similar task, asking several students to explain their current thinking, or surveying groups to see if their thinking changed after the exhibit. The key to this reflective process is checking the understandings that students have taken away from the learning episode and determining what knowledge they have constructed about the concept, process, or attitude being considered.

Recently we were consulting in a seventh-grade math class when the teacher was giving a lesson on circumference. The teacher reviewed two formulas for circumference, $c = \_\_ d$ and $c = 2 \_\_ r$. Students were to use these formulas after the diameter or the radius was given. Then two values for pi were provided, either 3.14 or $22/7$, and a discussion ensued about giving a measurement in either decimals or fractions. After surveying a majority of students as they worked the practice problems, we found that most of them had some understanding of calculating the answer but very little understanding of what pi is and how it is derived. This information surfaced from informal interactions rather than during formal reflection. We talked with the teacher about a follow-up lesson when students would investigate the relationship between diameter and circumference for a variety of circles. The reflective activity of analyzing student understanding based on considering the learning episode with your class is the most critical process in a CLD.

Teachers gather data about individual student understanding. Individual reflections offer teachers a look at student learning and data to document that learning. For instance, teachers often assume that they've covered certain material and that most of the students will take similar knowledge away from the classroom. This is seldom borne out by actual practice. Teachers can quickly see and hear the similarities and differences in the meaning that students have made of specific learning episodes and of entire units.

One example of gathering data during reflections is asking each student to make a schematic that captures her or his knowledge about the content in a curriculum unit. The schematic provides spaces to place key topics, related topics, topic flow, and key questions. As students complete this schematic, they graphically organize course information in ways that make sense to them as individuals. A teacher can then collect and review the schematic data to assess student understanding of the unit. The point is *not* for all the students to do it the same way! This is not an exercise like diagramming sentences but rather is an engaging activity that invites students to show how they connect the pieces of the material they are learning. We've had good success having students start individually, compare with a neighbor, and then present in pairs to the class. Schematics are also a terrific activity to do at the beginning of a learning episode.

An exhibit can reassure teachers that the curriculum they've adopted or designed is influencing student learning of regional, state, or national learning goals. Reflective activities can be aligned with these goals, offering appropriate data not only for teachers but also for their students and for other stakeholders. With the current reactionary movement toward standardized testing, teacher-designed assessment might seem less credible, but we believe that teacher-designed assessment and standardized testing will both document student learning from a CLD that is well thought out.

Teachers connect the learning episode to big ideas and address common misconceptions. Reflections offer the teacher a road map for going to the next step. Students may demonstrate a clear understanding of a topic that the teacher had intended to pursue further. Conversely, a concept, process, or attitude that the teacher thought students understood might not be understood, or might be misunderstood or partially understood. A subsequent learning design giving students another opportunity to revisit that topic can be shaped more effectively because teachers can refine their approach.

The schematic described above can include a *big idea,* which gives students a chance to write about the main idea of a unit or a reference to future learning of specific topics that students want to learn more about.

The future-learning aspect of the schematic gives the teacher good information about ways to proceed. And students feel they are valued when teachers use their suggestions.

Students individually consider their thinking during the learning episode. Individual reflections capture feelings, images, and ideas from the learning episode itself. Each learner makes different meaning and understanding of any learning event, and teachers can offer students systematic ways to capture those differences. Students can reflect aloud as they speak with a peer, to their study group, or to the full group. Students can reflect by writing on an index card, by responding to guiding prompts on a single sheet, or by jotting one thought on a sheet of butcher paper or an overhead transparency for the class to review. Students can also reflect privately in a journal and see patterns emerge over time.

Students can respond to a teacher's prompt, to another student's prompt, or can initiate the reflection themselves. Ideas in texts or other curriculum materials can be useful for framing reflective activities. Reflections on learning are as creative as an individual can make them. For instance, elementary students can reflect about a story just read by writing a different ending and then telling why they chose their ending. As in any thoughtful teaching, shape and structure improve students' chances for success rather than limiting opportunities. Reflective activities gain potency by building on the facilitator's strengths and values. Questions from the back of the chapter, deadly boring when presented as homework, can be reconfigured into opening gambits. Instead of, "Name the six continents that have trading partners," the prompt could be, "Look at a globe and figure out which continent is least likely to have trading partners, then draw a picture of someone who lives there and show it to the class." You might get a penguin phoning in for pizza or a scientist living in a research station studying snow. You will certainly get more engaged learning and increase the odds that every student will remember images of Antarctica.

Students record their thinking to document learning. Reflections can be used to document one's own learning over time. Although the exhibit generally focuses on learning within a specific event, systematic documentation of reflections can show change over time. Reflective metacognition, or making meaning of learning by thinking about thinking, can be done only as a systematic process with sustained effort. Engaging students in a regular process for analyzing their own thinking is integral to *learning to be a learner,* which many teachers see as the main purpose of education.

Reflections can be completely private, partially shared, or shared with the entire class. Obviously, the time available does not allow asking every student to speak in front of the whole group after every learning episode. Teachers must choose at what level students will make public their individual reflections. This choice is based on the quality of a learning episode, the need for individual accountability, the potential in a public sharing for inspiring or teaching others, and the use of data that will emerge from the sharing. Any teacher who strives on a regular basis to document what students learn knows the challenge of doing so during a busy day. Be selective to make the most of the students' energy and of the data students gather. Treating student data as an assessment of learning for both students and teachers and also as an evaluation of learning for a broader audience of parents and the school community, will encourage documentation.

Students revisit their thinking after the learning episode. As we taught and reflected on this last-but-not least element of the CLD, we realized that students do not quit thinking when they walk out the door of our classroom. We have assigned reflective papers as homework that encourage students to consider their own thinking. As we read their papers, we realized that many students took pains to judge their thinking during the learning episode. Some recognized the inertia of their own ideas and adopted new ideas presented by others. Others remained ambivalent about the subject or uncommitted to any particular idea. Students may be persisters, persuaders, or prevaricators—but they invariably continue to review the learning episode and to revisit their thinking about a topic long after the class is over. We all evaluate and reevaluate real-life learning experiences, too. For instance, we try to make sense out of winds, waves, and tides when we are sailing on the Sound, but we may learn what we did right or wrong only later when we revisit the experience in our imaginations and reflect on the theory we were trying to apply.

We now understand that that careful reconsideration must be acknowledged and made use of following an episode. When the next class convenes or the sailboat is put in the water, the press of the new agenda must not be allowed to push aside that careful reconsideration.

This realization confirms our commitment to reflections by both the class and individuals during a learning episode, because it can enhance the benefits of current considerations and set up students for ongoing analysis of their thinking and learning.

Examples of Reflections Elements

In this section, we offer examples of reflections from four CLDs taken from a dozen designs in the Resources section. These designs are intended for four levels of students. The primary (K-3) CLD is from reading and is about retelling *Brown Bear.* The intermediate (3-6) sample is from special education and is about vending machines. The middle school (6-9) example is from industrial arts and is about scooter motors. The high school (9-12) illustration is from business education and is about creating spreadsheets. We chose examples from four subjects to emphasize the utility of the CLD. Examine these four reflections and note that each requires teachers to arrange collective and individual considerations of student thinking during the learning episode. Then consider how each example aligns with our characteristics. Do teachers gather data about individual student's understanding, connect to big ideas, and address common misconceptions? Do students record their reflections and revisit their thinking? Compare the following examples (Figure 6.1) with these criteria and decide whether or not different reflections elements satisfy enough of our characteristics. After exploring these four examples, revisit the complete designs to see how they bring closure to a CLD.

Theory

Reflection is the act of describing to ourselves what we have already felt, seen, and talked about; how we are making new meaning, adding to our current understanding, or enhancing current knowledge within a learning episode; and what we will do or think more about because of that learning episode. One powerful example of reflective activity evident in our teaching is the thinking we do about the learning and teach-

FIGURE 6.1

Example Reflections Elements

Reflections 5 minutes	Primary Grades: Reading—Retelling the Story How does it feel to write a new book together? How did you choose the words to tell about your animal? How would you change the color or movement of your animal if we did this again?
Reflections 10 minutes	Intermediate Grades: Special Education—Vending Machines The teacher invites students to discuss their experiences. Why were you or weren't you successful? What would help you be successful next time? What are some characteristics of vending machines? What are some strategies that will help you use vending machines in the future?
Reflections 1 week to write, edit, and put on a web page	Middle School: Industrial Technology—Scooter Motor The teacher leads ongoing analysis of gas-engine repair based on problems that students encounter. What did you know about small gas engines at the beginning of the term? What was the most difficult concept to understand? How did you make sense of that concept, teach it to others on your team, or demonstrate that you now understood it? If you were to teach a class about small gas engines, how would you proceed? Given the movement away from use of small gas engines toward electric ones, is small gas-engine repair an important skill?
Reflections Last day	High School: Business Education—Creating Spreadsheets The teacher leads the class in considering the similarities and differences in group spreadsheets. In what categories did you expect to find the most income or spending? What surprised you most about the class's expenses or income? How would you use a spreadsheet to balance a checkbook?

ing process before a learning episode. As we shape or design a learning episode, we talk to ourselves or others about what we hope to accomplish. We consider our own knowledge, the content we are addressing, and the learners. We draw upon past experience with our own strengths as teachers, with the content and how it can be made accessible to learners, and with the group's history with that same content or related content. Based on our repertoire in each area, we use our judgment to frame the next experience.

Throughout a learning episode, we constantly measure, assess, and take stock of how the learners are interacting with the material. Tiny, incremental decisions are made within a web of newly emerging information and assumptions that we already hold about the content and the learners. Each learning episode provokes different responses to the learners as we seek the most productive way to move learners to the next level or layer of understanding.

At the end of each episode, we ask students to reflect on their own thinking as they were moving through the learning process. As they reflect and write about their thinking, they produce documentation of their learning. Often students tell us that they were not clear on the concept, process, or attitude until the class considered it together. Without the benefit of class consideration and their personal reflection, that realization might be discarded or ignored.

Finally, after the learning episode is completed, we relive the episode by refeeling the emotions, looking back at the images, and articulating the self-talk about our understanding of what went on. Newly strengthened with this information and the complex processes used to gather it, we proceed to the next learning episode.

Precedents

In an essay called "Why Reflective Thinking Must be an Educational Aim," John Dewey outlines three purposes of reflection. Reflection makes possible: (a) action with a conscious aim, (b) systematic preparations and inventions, and (c) enriched meaning. Maxine Greene (1995) has interpreted and presented the work of John Dewey in many of her articles. She writes that, "Learning, after all, is a reflected-on process that moves on into conscious *praxis* in an unpredictable world" (p. 68). Both Dewey and Greene focus on the pathway of knowledge from a lived experience, through reflection upon it, toward plans for the future. Many perspectives on the relationship of thinking to language are illuminating. Alex Kozulin's 1986 translation of Vygotsky's (1934) *Thought and Language* allows Western readers insight into his powerful thinking about the psychology of language. Vygotsky's description of inner thought suggests that cognition or knowing is a complex process that begins with an inner dialogue with one's self. Those people who support learners must understand this often-invisible form of reflection. Hans Furth (1966) reminds us that deaf students reflect through "thinking without language."

Schøn's work (1983) on reflection in action begins this chapter. Schøn studied the thinking of professionals including architects, psychotherapists, and engineers, and investigated how those in the professions articulate knowledge that has remained invisible or tacit. Richard

Schmuck (1997) in *Practical Action Research* talks about the need for educators to move in a cycle from reflection to inquiry to improvement. We agree with his belief that mature teachers focus on effective practice and seek strategies to improve student learning and to evaluate their success. Professionals act, reflect on those actions, and then act again. Without the systematic reflection suggested by both Schøn and Schmuck, improvement in practice remains elusive.

Narrative has become more widely understood and used in our field in the past two decades. Carol Witherell and Nel Noddings's (1991) edited volume *Stories Lives Tell: Narrative and Dialogue in Education* offers the student of education a rich volume about the usefulness of narrative. Whether through autobiographical reflection or by using the stories of others, teachers can tap deeply individual, personal reflection to connect student and teacher or student and idea. In *Handbook of Qualitative Research,* Jean Clandinin and Michael Connelly (1994) legitimized individual reflections as "personal experience methods." And they described the inquiry into narrative that is required if we are to become students of our own lives. In "Recherche: Teaching Our Life Histories," Collay (1998) explained how her research activities became a systematic method of engaging new teachers in reflection throughout their first year. As we have observed over many years, we teach who we are. It is essential that we stop and think about *whom* we are teaching to our students.

Jerome Bruner (1996) also took up the theme of narrative as reflection in *The Culture of Education.* He revisited his three modes of mental representation: Enactive is the representation of physical action; iconic is the representation of visual imagery; and symbolic is the representation of language, primarily. These three modes of representation echo our three symbolic systems of feelings, images, and languages. We agree that these three internal systems comprise the processes of thought. We argue that feelings and images are also symbolic systems and are not just modes of representation. Facial expressions and body language symbolize feeling, and icons without words are symbols that communicate across cultures. When students reflect on their own thinking and learning, we ask them to talk or write about their awareness of feelings, images, and languages as the symbolic systems we construct to represent external experience as internal thoughts.

Critical reflection also focuses on systematizing reflective practice and using the information or ideas that are revealed to improve practice or to make decisions. Steven Brookfield's (1995) *Becoming a Critically Reflective Teacher* emphasizes this strategy. He describes the importance of confronting our own assumptions or taken-for-granted beliefs lest we enact our praxis thoughtlessly. Jack Mezirow and associates (1990) published a series of articles about reflection and adult learning. *Fostering Critical Reflection in Adulthood* contains many useful ideas and shows reflection in many different contexts of personal and professional learning.

Metacognition is often described colloquially as thinking about thinking. *Meta* is the Greek word for *beyond* or *after,* and *cognition* is from the Latin word for *knowledge* and refers to the process of knowing in the broadest sense, including perception, memory and judgment. The whole process of reflection is directed to analyzing, synthesizing, and evaluating our thinking. These higher orders of thought are concerned primarily with the process of thinking itself and not with the recollection, comprehension, or application of information. We include both collective and individual reflections in our CLD because of the important role that metacognition plays in understanding and using what we experience and learn.

Teachniques for Reflections

Time and Space for Reflecting

Individual and collective reflections are a very important part of learning episodes. Often groups spend so much time on their explanations and presentations that little time is left for reflection. We recommend that you leave at least five minutes for personal reflection and at least ten minutes of class consideration time on days when learning designs are ending. Students' metacognitive activity should focus on what they were thinking as they were explaining the *situation.* We have found it helpful to describe thoughts as the feelings, images, and languages the students experienced as they were working with their groups. These reflective activities must be carefully structured so that each student is held accountable and their learning is documented.

Closing Circles

This closing activity is a quick and useful way to circle quickly around a classroom so each student says one thing they now know about the topic or how they intend to apply the new information. Sometimes called a whip, the prompt should ask students to speak about something they learned, something they still have a question about, something they will do differently as a result of the lesson, or any other topic that provokes assessment of new learning.

Index Cards

Students each write about their thinking on an index card and turn it in, or students tell another class member what they plan to do next to prepare their project. Index cards can be used for one response or used over time to collect initial plans, new information, and final thoughts about a project. For instance, a class is observing their group's process for three meetings. On 5- by 8-inch index cards, they first write their names, their role in the group, the number of members, and the configuration of furniture. Over time, they add new pieces of information and analyze changes as the group develops. They will also use that card to write up their final report. You can easily vary the length of the reflections by selecting smaller or larger index cards to suit the time available.

Journal Entries

Another prompt for reflections is asking students to make a single entry in their journal. For example, language arts students could write something they now know about the main character in a story or a question they have for the author of a book. Special education students could note what kind of currency they will need to buy lunch from vending machines or whom they would like to pair with for a trial. Fine arts students could describe a possible subject for a sketch or what color they would choose if they could only use one. Depending on the developmental level of the students, they can write or tell a teacher or another student about what they think and why.

Write a Letter to One's Self or to the Subject of Study

After class activities have given students opportunities to think about the topic at hand, writing a letter provides a personal and meditative activity for them. When students read a class play, they can choose one of the minor characters and write a letter to her or him from themselves. They can also write as one of the other characters to the main character of the play. Depending on the teacher's purpose, the letter can be structured to include content that is indicated by local or national standards.

Learning Circle Considerations

The most important role colleagues can play in supporting both the reflection in action described by Schøn and CLD reflections by students is to practice it themselves. We are convinced that the school culture of racing through content, teaching subjects in disconnected ways, and not teaching to real-life situations reduces opportunities for reflection, much less thoughtful, systematic reflection. How many teachers stop during or at the end of their day and think about how the lesson or day went? Few have the luxury of time, and fewer can make the changes needed to create such time. How many teachers give their students the same luxury of time and space to think about their learning? The culture of schools does not encourage or even allow time and support for reflection. Journaling along with your students is a great way to model learning and gain a few minutes to think.

Trading simple, easily accomplished reflective activities is another positive way to support colleagues and yourself. The five-minute closing circle can even be offered as a classroom management strategy for those fearful of stopping too soon. Trading reflective prompts between disciplines is also extremely helpful. As you borrowed the notion of journal keeping from writers, so too can you borrow traditions of reflection from other fields. For instance, students working their way through a step-by-step project such as creating a scene in a play can turn and tell a neighbor about one thing they plan to do the next day to prepare the scene.

Concluding Remarks

We often think of reflections as the *so what?* of the lesson, unit, or course. Least understood and most often overlooked, this final element is the reason we work so hard at all the other parts of the CLD. Students need a chance to say what they learned—if they can't, then the process of telling, and perhaps the learning itself, needs attention. You need a chance to hear what students say, especially when the learning is effective. You may seldom ask your students what they've learned because you are afraid of what they might say. We use careful language in this stage of our development so that we don't open ourselves to negativity or thoughtless criticism. For instance, if you ask students to write down something they now know about a topic, then they're likely to give a proactive response. If you ask students, "Did you learn anything?" then they might not give a positive response.

Our experience has been that expectations breed success. When you perceive students as knowledgeable and able contributors, they contribute. When you document those contributions and talk about their goodness, students are more likely to feel successful as learners. Feelings of success are simple but elusive. Students learn something most of the time, and they will tell you about their learning when you ask them about their thinking.

Chapter 7

Productive Assessment

Not Just a Closing Activity

Without question, an experienced, insightful teacher can provide the most accurate and revealing portrait of student growth. But a teacher's skill in evaluating students doesn't just happen. It must be learned.

—Ernest L. Boyer, *The Basic School* (1995, p. 110)

Teaching is a complex process of decision making based on continual assessment of classroom conditions, interpersonal relations, collaborative thinking, and individual learning. With the development of Goals 2000 during the early 1990s at the national level, and with many states adopting new graduation standards during the last decade, a new era of accountability in public education has arrived. Often this push for accountability has produced new state tests geared to graduation standards; the expectation is that students will explain their thinking as they decide on appropriate answers. This kind of high-stakes testing puts pressure on teachers and administrators to show that students are raising their scores. As a result, ineffective teachers are threatened with termination. The dilemma for classroom teachers is that preparation for annual assessment alone does not improve student learning. A variety of assessment approaches is required to create the portrait Boyer (1995) describes. Teachers seeking to represent students' learning in the most comprehensive way must incorporate assessment into their daily teaching by routinely examining student thinking. Only by clarifying how students make their own meaning and construct knowledge with others can teachers support individual and collective learning.

Assessment is an integral part of every step in the process of constructivist learning design. Teachers design a *situation* based on their assessment of students' needs, developmental levels, and interests. Teachers design a process for *groupings* based on their assessment of interpersonal processes, thinking styles, and materials. Teachers design a simple assessment of what students already know as a *bridge* to what they want students to learn. Teachers design *questions* to guide, clarify, and integrate student thinking in order to assess their understanding of the concepts, skills, or attitudes they are trying to learn. Teachers arrange an *exhibit* for students to record what they have thought and to present it to others for peer assessment of thinking. Teachers arrange for *reflections* on students' collective learning and thinking as a self-assessment of individual learning. We will describe in detail how assessment takes place in each element of CLD.

Situation Assessment

As you design and guide students through a *situation,* you must assess on several levels. First, assess what students need to learn. Consider the expectations of the community for your grade level or subject, outcomes specified in the district curriculum, any markers or checkpoints toward state graduation standards, and curriculum standards from professional organizations. These include the National Council of Teachers of Mathematics (NCTM), International Reading Association (IRA), National Council of Teachers of English (NCTE), National Science Teachers Association (NSTA), National Council of Social Studies (NCSS), and International Society for Technology in Education (ISTE). This alphabet soup of acronyms is most often decoded only by teacher educators or researchers in higher education who expect teachers to use national standards as they design curriculum and evaluation standards. Most teachers are aware of what children are expected to learn at any given grade level or in a particular curriculum and use those expectations as their benchmarks. They may not be aware of links between local and national standards.

Second, assess the developmental level of students both individually and collectively. You are constantly learning about the developmental status of students and what they are capable of understanding. Teachers have no quick inventories. They observe and make judgments about what students are thinking, and they measure that learning against a conceptual framework of appropriate development. Elementary school teachers assess whether their students are thinking perceptually or conceptually by analyzing their explanations. Are student explanations based on perceptions of sensory appearance or on mental concepts constructed through experience? A common standard for assessment is Piaget's (1969) classic description of conservation of number, length, mass, and volume as these emerge sequentially at about ages 7, 8, 9, and 10. Do students see things as equivalent based on their appearance or do they realize that appearances can be deceptive and conserve the quantity even if it appears to be transformed? Do students who are shown a wide short container and a narrow tall container, both of which hold an equal volume, think one of them holds more rice than the other? Secondary school teachers assess whether their students think through concrete or formal operations. Are their decisions based on acquired experiences or on logical structures? Do students think the height of a can of tennis balls exceeds its circumference?

Third, assess what captures the interest of your students or piques their curiosity. You know the culture of children or teenagers in our society: where they like to go, what they like to do, what's hot and what's not, who is in and who is out, and what the trends are in their world. You may also know about the personal lives of students. What is their home life like, how are they treated and supported by adults in their lives, what chores or jobs do they have, what sports or activities are they involved in, and what hobbies or interests do they pursue? Most of this background is gathered through informal conversations or interactions and is important information to consider as you arrange a learning situation.

Groupings Assessment

As you make decisions about *groupings* of students and materials, assess the interpersonal skills and thinking styles of your students and the appropriateness of available materials. First, assess the interpersonal skills of students as they interact, communicate, and work with other students in the class. Often, the way students enter a classroom, take a seat, talk with friends, or stow their gear tells a lot about their mood and attitude. Assess the confidence, attention, personality, and ability of students to relate with others as they carry themselves, engage in conversation with friends, exchange jokes or jibes, listen to others, dominate the conversation, or defer to peers. These observations provide useful information as you group students so they can think together effectively. You can form groups by random assignment early in a term until you get to know your students. Then you can hand-group them to put high talkers together and low talkers together so some students don't always dominate group thinking while others usually withdraw. Likewise, *quick studies* may be put together and so may *slow studies,* so more students can think things through for themselves. The same kind of separation of *worker bees* and *drones* might also be useful to encourage contributions from more students. These terms do not refer to students' capacity for intellectual work but rather to how they present themselves on a continuum. Each grouping decision can effect the quality of thinking between students in a group, and as a term moves along, you become more familiar with individuals and can arrange groups of students based on previous observations and decisions.

Second, assess the thinking styles of students so you can support their learning. Are students emotional thinkers who need to act before they can imagine or talk about their learning? Are students visual thinkers who need to watch others and observe their actions before they can act themselves or talk about their learning? Are students verbal thinkers who need to listen to descriptions and talk about their learning before doing it themselves or observing others? These standard kinds of assessment reduce complex theory to simple generalizations about symbolic systems, but you can use them to make decisions about how to engage students and understand their thinking to support learning. Putting students who have different thinking styles together often produces more creative and divergent thinking because different points of view, strategies, and ways of thinking are represented. Sometimes teachers put similar thinkers together and then compare the results of different groups. This deliberate choice of who works together in groups can influence the quality of collaborative thinking.

Third, assess the materials available to support students in making meaning and constructing knowledge. Many classrooms have a rich array of manipulative materials, art and office supplies, scientific instruments and equipment, maps, charts, and graphs, or computer-based technology and Internet access. Other classrooms have only textbooks, paper, and pencils. Talk with other teachers in the school to see what they have or where to get materials. Talk with the principal or the district curriculum coordinators to see what materials are available. Ask the PTA or PTO to fund sets of math models or science kits that can travel from room to room as needed. Use paper, pencils, and scissors to draw diagrams and cut out models. Be as creative as you can in finding ways for students to construct models or representations for concepts they are learning.

Jigsaws, or structuring group process so that each member's information or materials are necessary for the group to succeed, is a good way to move teacher and students away from the competitive model of school. Working independently and completing the assignment first will not serve most people in the workforce today. Our youth may not succeed in the real world with classroom-style competition as their model.

Bridge Assessment

One of our math colleagues was preparing to teach a learning episode on fractions to seventh graders. As a bridge to what they already knew, he asked them about selecting half of a cake if it was divided vertically or horizontally, as depicted in Figure 7.1.

The students agreed that both cakes were equal and divided in equal halves, but if they were going to select a half to eat, then they would choose the one on the right. It appeared larger to them because it was divided vertically. He talked with them about their concepts of a half and equal shares, and they attributed their thinking to how they perceived it to appear rather than to their concept of half.

FIGURE 7.1
Horizontal and Vertical Halves

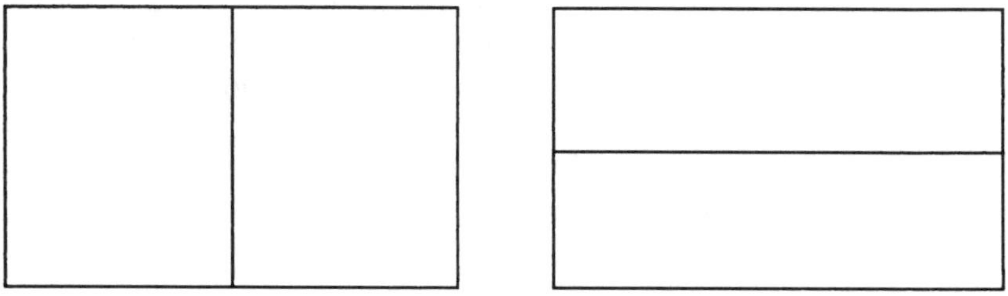

This kind of assessment about what students already know or think they know is very important to identify conceptions and misconceptions at the start of a learning episode. What students think and why they think so can have a profound effect on what they learn. Without conducting some basic, informal assessment about prior knowledge, you may search for a key in the dark. For example, we ask groups to sort out a simple problem such as the halves question, to have a group discussion, to play a game, to role-play a simulation, or to brainstorm a list of connections. Determining what students already know can be done quickly and yields information about prior knowledge for the teacher to use in making connections to the learning episode. Without this kind of simple assessment, it can be difficult to determine what is existing knowledge, what previous conceptions or misconceptions are interfering with making meaning about new ideas, how new ideas are being connected to previous knowledge, and what new knowledge is being constructed. These questions are at the heart of constructivist learning.

Some great ways to bridge between prior knowledge and new learning are these:

- In social studies, have students draw a map of a country, continent, or the world and fill in everything they can. After they study the material, have them draw the map again from memory.

- In science, ask students to decide what will happen if they test a scientific theory. For example, if they drop a ball of clay into a glass of water, then will the water level rise, stay the same, or go down? Then ask the students to change the experiment and predict the results. In the previous example, you could flatten the clay so it will sit on the surface of the water and ask students to decide again what will happen to the water level. Then have them conduct experiments to test their theories.

- In art, ask students to draw a human face and describe the relationship of eyes, ears, nose, and mouth on the face. Then look at faces in the class and consider the commonalities an artist might use in drawing portraits.

- In physical education, have students work in groups to create games with a basketball or soccer ball that require cooperation rather than competition to win.

- In math, ask students to count using only the numbers zero to four to surface what they know about place value in base five.

These are just some examples of using a bridge to assess what students already know about a concept, process, or attitude. If you think about ways they can show you rather than just tell you, then you have a record of their prior knowledge to compare to the knowledge they construct during a learning episode. They, too, have a record of their new learning and can effectively reflect on their thinking.

Questions Assessment

Assessment is probably most visible in this element. Many of the questions teachers ask, however, are not intended to assess students' knowledge but to guide, clarify, or integrate their thinking. The purpose of such questions is not to evaluate but rather to discern and understand student thinking. Instead of focusing on speed or accuracy in student responses, these questions are intended to assess the nature and quality of thinking that students are doing as they learn a concept, process, or attitude during a learning episode.

When teachers ask clarifying questions to discern and understand student thinking, several different kinds of assessment take place. Teachers are trying to get inside the heads of students and assess how students are making meaning and what understandings they are developing. This involves discerning what prior knowledge students brought with them, what new learning is taking place, and how their knowledge is being reconstructed. Teachers also assess what students are thinking, why students are thinking that way, and how they are responding to their own thinking. They are sorting out the concepts, processes, and attitudes embedded in the knowledge that students are constructing. Teachers further assess how students relate to others, communicate with others, and motivate themselves. Much of this assessment takes place informally as teachers observe the dynamics of small groups, decide when to participate or intervene in the group interaction, and ask questions to clarify group thinking.

When teachers ask integrating questions, a different kind of assessment is going on. These questions are more focused on bringing the students' collaborative thinking to a common or shared meaning among those in each group. They are preparing groups for a presentation of their thinking during the exhibit. Teachers determine if most of the students in a group understand the shared meaning by asking them for analysis, synthesis, and evaluation of that group's thinking by different students in the group. Those students most reluctant to participate may be the least able to articulate the group's thinking and shared meaning. Teachers also assess when to seek closure on accomplishment of a task and move forward to an exhibit of student artifacts and explanations.

Exhibit Assessment

The primary intent of an exhibit is for students to make their thinking visible so that they and their teacher can assess their learning. This is different from just asking for the correct response or explanation. The more we value speed and accuracy in memorizing facts no matter what the subject, the less we communicate to students that their thinking is important. We refer to the product students create to show their thinking to others as an *artifact*. This artifact should record or document their thinking together about the task they have to accomplish. The students present these artifacts, and the teacher examines them to determine how students are thinking and tries to assess what they understand and know about the concept, process, or attitude that the learning episode is addressing. These two events are at the heart of assessment in an exhibit. First, have the students create an artifact that shows what they are thinking. Second, examine the artifact to assess student understanding and decide what is necessary to support student learning.

The ways that teachers ask students to exhibit their thinking is a crucial piece of the CLD. What would be a good /useful project for students that would also show you how they are thinking? For instance, you may want them to draw a diagram to solve a math or physics problem. In other cases, you may ask them to write a paragraph or essay describing an era or a character in social studies or language arts. Maybe you want them to brainstorm a list or develop criteria for identifying types of species or part of speech in science or language arts. One very interesting task is to create a metaphor of a structure or organization by using tinker toys, building blocks, or poster paper and markers. Hilda Taba (1971) offered this approach to linking topics or developing taxonomies in her inductive approach to social studies teaching. Sometimes we have students write ideas on Post-it notes and then put them on poster paper to create categories. Often in math, we ask students to show the problem, the solution, and their relationship by constructing representations with manipulative models. Sometimes we ask them to write or draw their information on an overhead transparency or on a white board. Other times we may ask students to display their computer work for the class.

The key to all of these exhibits is that students actually produce something in class that we can examine to assess their thinking. We don't just send them off with homework but have an example of their understanding to use in supporting their learning or designing more learning episodes. To determine what adult students of teaching knew about rational numbers, we gave them a problem and then asked them to solve it by drawing diagrams rather than using numbers or algebra. The problem was about Planet Xiar where two thirds of the men were married and half of the women were married. All marriages were between men and women. Students determined what fraction of the whole population represented unmarried men. As students presented the diagrams they created to solve this problem, a common theme emerged in their thinking. They decided that one half and two thirds of the same whole left one sixth of the population as unmarried men. They clearly were taking different parts of the same whole without considering that the men and women represented different wholes. At that point, we introduced solutions from other students who had thought about the problem in a different way, and students reconsidered their thinking.

Student-generated artifacts are the basis for assessment. These artifacts offer the teacher a window into students' minds as they were thinking about the situation. The presentation of their artifacts may not be what the teacher expected, but it does document their thinking for the teacher to assess and use in deciding where to go next. The framework of textbook-driven instruction is to assign daily homework and then test at the end of a section or chapter. For most students, this is way too late for assessment to do much good. Teachers can watch students work on a task and see how they are thinking during class. When we give our students an assignment to work on individually or in groups, we circulate around the classroom and look over their shoulders to see what they are producing or listen in to their conversations as they discuss the situation or explain their thinking to one another. When we asked our students of teaching to use this CLD as a framework for thinking about their own teaching, we could readily observe those who were comfortable specifying a purpose and a task for students to accomplish. Some panicked, others chose very general purposes, and still others selected an activity with no underlying purpose. These immediate and informal assessments guide our questioning and timing as we move the learning episode toward an exhibit of the artifacts that students create as they accomplish the task framed in a situation.

Perhaps the most powerful assessment is when students present their own thinking during the exhibit and then listen to others explain their thinking about the same task. The alternate perspectives offered in this exhibit element create the kind of feedback students need to learn more sophisticated ways to assess their thinking. Students will listen carefully to one another and respond to suggestions from peers more openly than if the teacher said the same things. Hearing a series of presentations also broadens student understanding of especially complex ideas—often they discover more than one way to resolve an issue, interpret a poem, or solve a problem. As a succession of artifacts is presented, that lesson is learned in a most powerful way.

Reflections Assessment

Reflections really involve two different kinds of assessment. The first kind is the public or group reflection to consider the explanations of thinking made during the exhibit. The teacher may draw the learning episode to a close and bring students to a common understanding of the concept, process, or attitude addressed in the situation. As students raise their questions or objections, teachers assess their understanding again and support them in struggling to make collective meaning from shared meaning.

The second kind of reflection is the analysis of personal thinking usually solicited in writing as a capstone to a learning episode. This reflection is a more private analysis when compared to the public consideration of individual or collaborative thinking presented during an exhibit. Teachers are able to assess how individual students were thinking as they worked to accomplish the task and present their thinking. This appropriate assessment of personal thinking also demands a great deal of honesty and trust from the students, respect and empathy for the learner from the teacher, and integrity from both the teacher and student. When we ask students to think about the feelings, images, and languages they experienced in their thinking, we are moving the relationship between teacher and student to a different level. Only by opening our thinking to others can we clearly examine our strengths and weaknesses. Teachers who get into the heads of students assume an awesome responsibility to be careful, patient, and supportive of learning. As students reveal their thinking, it is incumbent on teachers to assess this thinking and to assess how their misunderstandings can be clarified and guided to new thinking in a productive and positive way. So how students think, make meaning for themselves, and construct knowledge with others must all be assessed, accepted, and applied to support their learning. Both kinds of reflections offer another opportunity for teachers to assess the thinking and learning of their students.

Collecting individual reflections is a critical piece of the assessment puzzle. The index card comments we often collect at the end of a learning episode give us a quick glance at what students took away or what still confuses them. Many times we have notes from students indicating that they are still struggling with the concept, process, or attitude addressed by the situation, or they comment on the difficult time they had revisiting a previous assumption to consider a new understanding or way of thinking.

Learning Circle Considerations

The compelling need for ongoing, proactive assessment is a powerful topic to consider with your learning circle. The practice of informal seat-of-the-pants assessment is based on tacit knowledge of many teachers. They just do it and have little opportunity to think about how or why they do it. Individual beliefs about assessment practices in teaching are rich topics to discuss with colleagues. Assessment is especially significant in the current climate of high-stakes accountability in education. Teachers must articulate the variety of assessments they do through observing students, listening in on conversations, being aware of events in students' families and settings outside of school, and using their sixth sense to sort out when students are down or discouraged. These assessments may have more influence on the decisions you make about guiding, questioning, and supporting students during a learning episode than all of the chapter, state, and standardized tests put together. Perhaps the most important parts of our teaching are the subjective and personal judgments we make on a daily basis about the best ways to support student learning.

Local and national assessment of student learning is complex, statistics are often misinterpreted and misused, and any assessment is politicized. Classroom teachers and school leaders must walk a fine line between advocating for their students and responding to their constituents. We cannot offer readers reassurance that our design or any other will lead to higher test scores, nor can we in good conscience support the idea that higher test scores represent better learning. We encourage all teachers to discuss the best and most useful ways to structure the learning-teaching experience so that both teacher and students are confident that learning is taking place.

Concluding Remarks

Assessment takes place before, during, and after a learning episode as you make decisions about how to engage and support student learning. In this chapter, we addressed how assessment is considered in designing each element of a learning episode and then plays out as a teacher actually teaches a design. We have grown to value the information that teachers gather from students in a variety of ways, particularly because they use this information to make immediate decisions about what to teach, when to teach, and how to teach a concept, process, or attitude. We know that the results of these decisions and those made in the course of thinking through a CLD will unfold in the experience of actually teaching a learning episode based on our process of constructivist learning design.

Conclusion

Teaching Learning Designs

It is one of the great truths that what it is impossible to teach the child through words will be learned easily through the language of movement.

—Isadora Duncan, *The Art of the Dance* (1926, pp. 118-119)

Constructivist learning episodes actively engage students in a purposeful *situation* that involves collaboratively formulating questions, explaining phenomena, addressing complex issues, or resolving problems. *Groupings* of students make their own meaning of these tasks and actively construct knowledge together as the teacher asks guiding, clarifying, and integrating *questions*. Then students *exhibit* their accomplishment of the task. Finally, the teacher leads class and individual *reflections* about students' thinking as they made personal meaning, shared meaning, and collective meaning during the learning episode.

In this section, we first describe how a constructivist learning design unfolds chronologically or is taught during a learning episode. Then we revisit the fairy tales CLD presented in the first chapter to give details about how one CLD unfolded in different ways. We conclude with our reflections on learning about CLD. We present these descriptions using the metaphor of a dance rehearsal or production. We believe the parallels between choreographing a dance and designing for learning are apparent.

Dancing a Design

Teaching a learning design is like rehearsing a dance production. The teacher is both choreographer and leading dancer as she or he plans the sequence of elements in CLDs. A choreographer has danced in many recitals, studied with many great dancers and choreographers, listened to thousands of pieces of music, and directed many productions. Choreographers, like teachers, know their own likes and dislikes; choose from among available musical scores or commission a musical score; choose the venue; decide how best to use the space, time, and materials; and then begin rehearsing with the troupe. Choreographers have their own ideas about how things should work, but only when they see their dancers in action do they know how the dance will actually look. The dancers are the production, and they are not puppets responding to simple commands. At the end of the performance, they will feel like stars and get the credit for the beauty of the dance.

Choreographers and teachers have much in common. Each has choices to make and limitations to overcome. They both work to their own strengths and with the abilities of the troupe or students. They choose music or curricular approaches best suited to their groups, but they expect a certain level of skill and performance from each member. Some individuals are stars, whereas others are part of the dance line. Both dancers and students will know the repertoire of basic steps, but they will need coaching and modeling to move to the next level of performance.

Pacing, Rhythm, and Footwork

The performance art involved in leading a dance troupe or teaching a learning design depends on pacing, rhythm, and footwork. A dance production succeeds or fails if these are not precise, and they are just as important in constructing a successful learning episode. Both choreography and teaching require the careful development of a design, and each requires making quick judgments and decisions as the dance or learning episode unfolds. Pacing is highly variable and reflects the rhythm of each successive element in your design. When you begin the dance of a learning episode, how you describe the purpose and task of the situation to your students depends on many variables. The students' presence, mood, and attention are all factors in the decision. Sometimes, a burning social issue needs to be addressed, and other times, house-keeping chores need to be done. When you form groups and where you position them in the room are also considerations. A good production needs props and costumes. A good choreographer knows how to inspire the dancers by having them feel the rhythm as they rehearse. How you arrange materials beforehand, have students collect materials for a group, or distribute materials to groups are all matters of pacing. Any rehearsal or practice has its own tempo so that performers use their energy well and have something left at the end. When you begin the warm-up or *bridge* and how long you continue it is another variable. When you draw the task to a close and decide most students are ready to exhibit their work is also a question of pacing. At the end of each rehearsal, performers meet in the greenroom and take notes from the rehearsal leader, director, or choreographer. The focus of these notes or reflections varies depending on how much time is left to complete a learning episode. All of these decisions require watching the clock and managing time, minute to minute or hour to hour.

Footwork is the artistic part of teaching a learning design, the dance between students and teacher that you improvise as you go along. The modern dance that is a learning episode choreographed by a teacher is more fluid than a ballet because students dance to the same music in different ways from one day to the next. As a teacher, you find that the dynamic interplay between dancers and choreographer keeps you on your toes in responding to the unique rhythm of student performers. Students are not just spectators but are also participants in the performance art of creating a dance that you have choreographed. They are guided by your design but are encouraged to interpret and improvise. How you question students, how you decide to engage with a group, whom you choose to question, how you set up exhibits, whom you invite to reflect, and how you respond to students are footwork in the performance design. As in a dance production, we find that the order in which members or groups present can have a profound effect on the quality of the presentations. For instance, if the teacher starts the individual presentations by calling on a low-talking student who has a unique perspective on the solution to the problem, subsequent students will be more inclined to risk sharing their creative answers. If you ask each person to present, then all opinions are equal and not just those of high talkers with raised hands are recognized. A creative choreographer will shape the performance so that all dancers present themselves at their best.

Many teachers practice the performance art of teaching using deep, tacit professional knowledge acquired through long experience. Words on a page cannot express the dynamic interchange that evolves in seconds and minutes in each classroom. A dance recorded on paper does not suggest the personal dynamics among dancers during a performance. Similarly, no written learning design can possibly capture or predict the nuances of personal and emotional reactions that take place during a learning episode between students or between students and teacher. The nature of being a professional is that you make decisions quickly with little time to reflect on each choice but with confidence in your judgement.

Choosing Music for the Dance

Our CLD can be applied in any subject for classes or units of any size. Like choosing music for a dance, teachers must consider tempo and style as well as length of a learning episode. For example, composition teachers might ask students to construct the simplest sentences and compare their structure. Literature teachers might ask students to explain the motives of a character. Social studies teachers might ask students to assume the roles of two adversaries in a meeting. Science teachers might demonstrate a phenomenon and ask students to explain what was observed. Math teachers might ask students to find examples of sloping lines in the world around them—before introducing grids to determine equations. Foreign language teachers might engage students in conversational immersion without resorting to English translations. Art teachers might ask students to transform clay with their hands without looking at it. Music teachers might ask students to notate rhythms in a piece of music using their own symbols. The constructivist approach can be adapted to any subject area or curriculum by engaging students as active participants in making meaning and constructing knowledge. Successful students are never passive recipients of information given to them by the teacher.

The CLD can be incorporated into 45- or 50-minute class periods, 100-minute block schedules, and half- or whole-day sessions to teach a particular concept, process, or attitude. A single bridge or grouping of students for projects may apply to a unit that lasts two days or three weeks. These two elements can take a few minutes if the CLD lasts for one class period, or can take a day or more if the CLD is a unit. The bridge can be the first class session in a two- or three-week unit to ground students firmly in their own thinking before they begin work on a long-term task such as a case study, a project report, or a fine-arts production. Other learning episodes may present each element on a daily basis but link them together to teach concepts in a chapter or piece of literature. We often design three-hour morning or afternoon sessions with a single CLD and include more than one task to accomplish so that students move through a sequence of related tasks that increase in complexity. Sometimes, we develop designs for a weekend retreat or a weeklong institute with several different teachers.

Rehearsing the Dance

The six elements of CLD unfold in sequence as you rehearse the dance during a learning episode. You may make decisions to change the sequence as you engage with students and materials. But the sequence of elements that we propose contains more logic than magic. In our CLD, the six elements are in the order in which they will be rehearsed. First, announce the purpose and task you framed in the situation to your students. These are the *big ideas* that guide your rehearsal. This can be the most difficult element of learning design for new teachers. Clarifying the big ideas, determining a worthwhile task, and engaging students in some kind of inquiry around these ideas is not an easy process. As with most things, experience is the greatest teacher.

The second element in the learning episode is *groupings*. Your design considered how students might think collaboratively and what materials might support their thinking. Arranging groupings takes careful planning, too. "Put the kids in groups" is advice sometimes given to a teacher who is unprepared and needs a quick fix. Creating groupings, however, requires a different kind of preparation and is sophisticated teaching. We urge you to think about forming groupings of students and materials in advance so you don't spend valuable time during the learning episode deciding how to organize the groups and scrambling for materials. Students do have to get up, get their gear, move around to find their places, and settle into new groups. If the classroom contains flexible tables and chairs rather than individual desks, then forming and getting into groups is easy. We have set up groups with great furniture, bad furniture, and no furniture at all, so don't let classroom conditions become a barrier to working in groups.

We usually arrange students in groups before the bridge element because we find that the group interaction required to surface prior knowledge is a good warm-up exercise. The same or a subsequent group of students can then think and work together to accomplish a task. Our own experience, as well as a long tradition of research, demonstrates the value of small-group process for the social construction of knowledge. Many of our teacher colleagues prefer to build a bridge with the whole class and then organize the groups to accomplish their task. A large- or small-group bridge works equally well but nets different information for the teacher and has a different effect on the students. For instance, if you ask each dyad to share essays, it can be done quickly, and you can see immediately who has the work done. With groups of four or five, the sharing takes longer, but the breadth of ideas is greater. Reporting back from fewer groups takes less time, but the entire class hears fewer ideas. Large-group sharing must be carefully managed. You must choose wisely who speaks or you'll hear only from the usual high talkers.

The third element to play out in a learning episode is the bridge. We prefer to have students work in groups to reveal what they already know about the concept, process, or attitude addressed by the situation. Such collaborative thinking usually stimulates more discussion and raises a broader range of ideas than individual thinking. Sometimes we have students reflect privately about their prior knowledge. This strategy is effective for students who are not comfortable speaking out even in the smallest group, and individual documentation offers baseline data for each student. In any case, this strategy can be used periodically for formative assessment. Small-group conversations offer a safe way for students to express their ideas and test their thinking with others, especially if community-building activities have built a strong foundation of trust. In both cases, start with a prompt or question about the topic that will generate some data for the students and for yourself. Give groups a simple activity such as a problem, list, or game instead of merely asking a small group to discuss the topic. These activities generate real documentation, offer a more thorough introduction and review, engage more students, and don't take any longer than a discussion. Specific activities and required documentation reduce the time students spend chatting about unrelated topics. How you and your students build a bridge is not as important as doing it early in the learning episode so students can connect prior knowledge to new learning.

The fourth element to unfold during your rehearsal or learning episode is questions. During the design phase, you decided how you will ask guiding questions, anticipate student questions, respond with clarifying questions, and prepare integrating questions. Good questions lie at the heart of the CLD because they help you envision what students might think and do as they accomplish the task. As with any dance, the more time spent in design, the better the rehearsal can unfold. The key is to expect the unexpected and to cherish divergent thinking that emerges from students. Teachers need to be flexible and embrace the decision making that redirects the course of a learning episode. As in a dance performance, some movements may not convey your feeling, but different movements may do so equally well. Some groups take a long time, whereas other groups finish quickly and may need an additional task or focus, so you might have some content-related sponge activities at the ready. Groups moving more quickly can be prompted to the next level of thinking or can explore a tangent rather than languishing with nothing to do. The quickest groups may have the least thoughtful conversations. They can be prompted to revisit a part of the learning episode that was missed the first time around. We may move the learning episode toward closure before some groups are ready because they will benefit from listening to what others have thought and done. Some classroom management concerns still arise and need to be resolved, but when more students are engaged in thinking and learning together, fewer management issues emerge. You can encourage longer deliberation by rewarding thorough documentation. If completion of the task is valued but the quality of each student's learning is not, then the message is that high-quality learning is not important.

The fifth element to unfold in teaching a learning episode is the exhibit. This opportunity for students to show their work provides a record of their thinking, gives them a sense of satisfaction, and reassures you about what and how students are learning. We often use physical models, visual representations, index cards, sticky notes, poster paper, overhead transparencies, and different colored markers so each group can have a simple way to record and display their work. The materials the students use to document their accomplishment of the task must be readily accessible in the classroom. Prepare for this exhibit as you create a CLD. Sometimes, forms or copies need to be run off ahead of time, but usually, students learn more if they have to decide themselves on the structure and format for their presentation. Some groups will conceive of the task in very different ways from those you imagined, but students benefit from divergent thinking. Timing the exhibit can be a challenge. Groups complete their tasks at different times, and some may not be ready to present their work when others are. Because of questions from other students, presentations may take longer than you planned. You must decide when to proceed to an exhibit and allow enough time for reflections afterward. New teachers may rush through a learning episode to include everything rather than just postponing the exhibit and reflections until the next class session. They risk not including these elements at all because of pressure to move on and cover the next section. Consolidate episodes by choosing a shorter task, or link a series of tasks to the same bridge, exhibit, and reflections. Learning episodes lasting a week or more could have a single reflection session on Friday, but presenting and reflecting on accomplishments every day connects new learning with prior knowledge.

The sixth and last element during a learning episode is reflections. This is truly a case of last but not least! Students need time to critically reflect on their thinking throughout the learning episode. As students move through the cycle from making personal meaning to making shared meaning to making collective meaning, reflection on their thinking is necessary to complete the social construction of knowledge. Reflections contain two major parts. In the first part, lead a large-group consideration of how the learning episode unfolded. Revisit the big ideas; link this episode with previous ones; make connections and applications; challenge misconceptions that became evident during the exhibit; and commend minority opinions to show that minority views are heard and legitimized. During the second part of reflections, individual students make sense of their learning. Ask students to write, draw, or represent in some other way their individual thinking during the learning episode. This personal documentation creates time and space for students to communicate the feelings, images, and languages they experienced throughout the learning episode and allows you to hold individual students accountable. You may pick up on confusion, frustration, or satisfaction with their thinking that was not apparent during the learning episode itself. This final phase of the learning episode is a capstone experience that should bring together the elements of your CLD into a coherent whole or make you aware that this did not happen for some students. Making time and space for whole-group and personal *reflections* on thinking is essential.

A Tale of Three Dancers

The same choreography or learning design can be danced or taught in many ways depending on your interpretation. In the first chapter, we presented a fairy-tales CLD designed by three teachers and told their composite story of teaching this learning design. Now we revisit their story with more detail about how each taught her own version of this CLD. The situation element of the CLD focused on engaging students in analyzing fairy tales. They explained to students that their purpose was to understand the core elements and common themes that define this area of literature. Their ongoing purposes of strengthening writing, improving reading ability, and teaching study skills were also maintained throughout the CLD.

In the fairy-tales CLD, each teacher took a different approach to groupings. Ellen grouped the students randomly by handing out slips of paper with characters from several well-known fairy tales on them and asked the students to find the others whose characters were from the same story. This activity was fun for the students and tested their knowledge of the general literature. Gail grouped by location in the room. She was confident her class would be productive in almost any configuration. Sue had her students meet in writer's workshop learning circles, which she had set up earlier in the term.

Ellen, Gail, and Sue required students to complete the same prewriting activity. In the fairy-tales CLD, students first wrote individual reflections about a fairy tale from their own experience. This bridging activity allowed students to share thinking already begun, rather than asking them to consider a question for the first time. Ellen had had her students complete the prewriting activity the previous Friday because she had a substitute that day. Gail and Sue had their students write at home the night before. Bridge activities can take several forms, and some teachers use more than one in a learning episode. In teaching the fairy-tales CLD, all three teachers used three different bridge activities. First, all these teachers asked their students to write a reflection paper about memories of hearing a fairy tale. The essay served as a bridge for individual students to connect their prior knowledge to the task of identifying characteristics of fairy tales. During the class period, we observed Ellen telling a story about her grandfather's stories as a bridge to that day's activities, whereas Gail called on some of her students to share what they had written. In a third classroom, Sue put her students in their regular writer's workshop groups immediately and asked them to talk about their essays in those groups. She used writer's workshop strategies familiar to the students by having them critique one another's opening paragraph and offer suggestions.

The groups in each classroom behaved quite differently from one another and from those in the other two classrooms. Ellen's newly formed random groups bantered in a friendly competition to see which group could list the most characteristics commonly found in fairy tales. She stopped them after about 10 minutes and asked the students to debate the question of quality versus quantity that was evident on the butcher paper. Some of Gail's fairy tales groups worked quickly on the list of characteristics, with little discussion, whereas other groups took more time debating the goodness of various characteristics. She asked the most efficient groups to apply their characteristics to *Snow White and the Seven Dwarfs* because it had just been rereleased and most of the students had seen the movie. Sue's groups spent most of their time editing one another's opening paragraph and spent only a few minutes on the task of generating characteristics. Questions in each of the three classrooms ranged from "What is a characteristic?" to "Does this group's very long list contain more useful information than another list created by a group whose members spent more time debating the entries?" All three teachers asked individual students they knew to be low talkers to name a fairy tale and one of its characteristics.

Ellen and Gail got to the exhibit during the same day, whereas Sue put the exhibit off until the next day. Her writer's workshop groups needed more time to generate characteristics. Ellen's classroom is small, and the chart paper sheets were easily visible from every seat. The group recorder talked about the list and how it was generated. In Gail's classroom, the wall with room for chart paper is not easily seen from the desks, so small groups toured the room and examined each list. Gail asked each group to note which characteristics were consistent across all or most sheets. In all three rooms, some of the characteristics listed on the groups' chart paper were not valid. In Ellen's classroom, for example, the students themselves questioned other groups about whether "death of the lead character" was really a characteristic of all fairy tales. Gail revisited that debate after all groups had presented their exhibit and asked her students to place sticky dots on the characteristics that appeared on each sheet. Sue talked about the writing process and how students had used their writer's groups to clarify their thinking.

In teaching the fairy-tales CLD, each teacher added something to the reflections they designed. They all had their students read articles on fairy tales and compare the definitions and characteristics that the class had developed with those listed by the experts. In addition to writing about two questions for the next day, Ellen had students link back to the characters in their prewriting activity. She asked students to analyze their group's fairy tale using three characteristics from their new lists. Gail had students write down something that they would include when they wrote an original fairy tale. Sue had her students draft the next section of their writing assignment, a sketch of the plot of their original fairy tale. They each described how the teacher trio had designed the CLD, what they anticipated for the learning episode, and their interpretation of how it had come out. Each teacher told her class that the teachers would meet afterward, review the videotapes, and compare notes.

Dancing Together

One of the great joys we have as teachers is working together on creating a CLD and coteaching it so we can witness and discuss how the learning episode we imagined unfolded in real life. Every teaching episode we design and rehearse is an adventure. As in most creative endeavors, sometimes it succeeds beyond our wildest expectations and sometimes it flops miserably. Most of the time we see some things that worked well and some things we would change if we did it again. The process of creating a CLD with a colleague can be a wonderful experience. Most of you are not able to share your teaching with a colleague on a regular basis. Because teaching is usually a solo performance, we also tend to view planning for teaching as a solitary act. But designing for learning can be like dancing with a partner.

Often, planning is done spontaneously while taking a shower, while driving a car, or while reading student papers after our children are in bed. The opportunity to think together about our teaching is seldom part of our school culture. You spend preparation time planning lessons, organizing materials, or squeezing out a few minutes to manage your personal lives. Meeting times are spent on school business, district procedures, or curriculum professional development. Few graduate-degree programs focus on the process of teaching and learning.

We encourage you to find a teacher colleague to create one CLD with you. Invite a member of your department or grade-level team to think about how you both might teach a learning episode. The CLD language we use might not be familiar to your colleagues. You can talk with them about how they would find out what students already know or how students would present their work during a lesson rather than using the terms *bridge, exhibit,* and *learning episode.* We use different language because we have reframed the procedure of planning for teaching to a process of designing for learning. We realize that the new language may form a barrier for some teachers, and during conversations, our language isn't as consistent as it can be when writing. Many of our colleagues refer to constructivist *lesson* design and make other connections with previous planning formats that they have used effectively. We see them making their own meaning, and we never insist on uniformity as they struggle to understand the nuances of new language.

To get started, select a concept, process, or attitude you intend to teach in about a month, and share your understanding of how to create a CLD with your colleague. Think through the CLD elements in sequence and then imagine how your choices might play out with students. Imagine a couple of different situations, groupings, or bridges, and anticipate the effects of each one. How can you get the results you want? Do you foresee any problems with particular students or topics? After you agree on a CLD, try it out in your classes. Observe one another's teaching if possible, and then revise the design based on your observations and on student feedback. The give and take of going through the process of creating and improving a CLD with a colleague is professional collaboration at its best.

We found a focus on colleagueship similar to ours in *The Teaching Gap* by James Stigler and James Hiebert (1999). These educational researchers analyzed videotapes from math classrooms in the United States, Germany, and Japan that were recorded as part of the Third International Mathematics and Science Study (TIMSS). They learned that "teaching is not a simple skill but rather a complex cultural activity that is highly determined by beliefs and habits that work partly outside the realm of consciousness" (p. 103). They contend that teaching is so constant in our culture that we can't imagine or believe it should be changed and that educational reform efforts fail because most have little if any effect on actual classroom teaching. These researchers advocate a process of "lesson study" they adapted from the Japanese *jugyou kenkyuu*. Teams of teachers work on developing, piloting, observing, and revising a single "research lesson" for several months until they feel it improves student learning. Our suggestions in this section are echoed by their concept of collegial lesson study to improve the quality of teaching and learning in schools.

After designing a CLD together, look for opportunities to actually teach a learning episode together. Our teaching culture is quite solitary in all levels of education, with the best teaming evident in elementary schools. We find that teachers seldom take the time to observe their colleagues teach a class or lesson. Perhaps preschool teachers have the greatest camaraderie and collaboration because more than one teacher usually works with a group of children. If you can teach a CLD that you have developed together, it may be less intimidating or threatening to have your collaborator watch you teach. Usually teachers take responsibility for different elements of the learning episode, so one is teaching while the other is observing group process and student reaction. When you teach that CLD to another class, you might switch roles and teach the elements you watched before. You tend to get a better feel for the flow of the CLD as it unfolds during a learning episode from the inside looking out rather than from the outside looking in.

Inviting Administrators to the Dance

You may need to educate your principals about the process of CLD and what they should expect to see when they observe the flow of a learning episode. Most principals are working from an older model of instruction and supervision. They may not know constructivist learning theory or understand how its principles can be applied to engage students in learning. Thinking in groups, surfacing prior knowledge, accomplishing tasks without specific instruction, displaying learning, and reflecting on thinking may all be new constructs for building administrators to consider in evaluating teachers. These issues need to be addressed in the preconference and reviewed in the postconference so that your principal is clear about your teaching methodology and learning expectations. Your classroom and teaching style may look much different from any a principal anticipates without this preparation and debriefing.

Inviting Others to the Dance

We hope you enjoyed reading our book and will appropriate some ideas for your teaching. We thought and learned more about the process of constructivist learning design than we ever expected. We clarified our own understanding about different elements in the social construction of knowledge. The power of reflecting and writing together as vehicles for our own thinking and learning was reaffirmed for us. Our metaphor has been one of labor and delivery. The last 10% of the process took as much energy as the first 90%. The time may have been compressed but the experience was intense. As we sat together at one computer going through the chapter drafts and doing revisions line by line, the quality and clarity of writing improved tremendously. We also learned the true meaning of *collaboration* or laboring together. Thank you for being part of the class for our exhibit of thinking. We would be pleased if you shared your reflections as a reader with us, offered your own CLDs for other teachers to consider, or analyzed a learning episode. Visit our Web site at www.prainbow.com/cld to post your reflection, design, or analysis.

Resources

RESOURCE MATRIX

CLD Matrix for Examples of Elements (Chapters)			
Level	Situation (1) & Questions (4)	Groupings (2) & Exhibit (5)	Bridge (3) & Reflections (6)
Pimary Grades *Resources 1, 2, 3*	Fine Arts *Drawing Animals*	Physical Education *Imitating Animals*	Reading *Retelling the Story*
Intermediate Grades *Resources 4, 5, 6*	Science *Moon View*	Media Technology *Logo*	Special Education *Vending Machines*
Middle School *Resources 7, 8, 9*	Language Arts *Fairy Tales*	Mathematics *Base Blocks*	Industrial Technology *Scooter Motor*
High School *Resources 10, 11, 12*	Social Studies *Trading Partners*	Foreign Language *Spanish Songs*	Business Education *Creating Spreadsheets*

RESOURCE 1

Level: Primary Grades
Subject: Fine Arts
Title: Drawing Animals

Situation *50 minutes*	The purpose of this sequence of three *situations* is for young students to make further meaning of the rhythmic, patterned story *Brown Bear, Brown Bear, What Do You See?* "Brown bear, brown bear, what do you see? I see a yellow duck looking at me." They engage in rich literature activities by listening to the story or song, drawing new animals, writing a parallel phrase, acting out new behaviors, describing these new behaviors in words, and retelling the story through new pictures and words. Students choose a new animal and a color for that animal. Each individual or group creates a page for a book about new animals. The teacher or assistant collects the sheets into a book and has students write on their page the story pattern for that new animal and color.
Groupings *3 minutes*	A. To create work groups, students pull from a basket an index card naming one of nine animals in the original story. B. Materials such as markers, crayons, construction paper, drawing paper, and glue are available for the groups to depict their invented animals. Students can create one picture per child or one per group.
Bridge *5 minutes*	The teacher reads *Brown Bear, Brown Bear, What Do You See?* to the children. Some teachers might create a simple melody and sing the story. The teacher asks the children to listen for the various types and colors of animals "looking at me."
Questions *20 minutes*	The teacher reads *Brown Bear, Brown Bear, What Do You See?* again. This time, the teacher asks, "What other animal could we put here, and what color could it be?" Students are encouraged to be inventive and not criticize "polka-dot salamanders." Student: "Should I make my parrot green like the picture book or a new color?" Teacher: "Is your animal real or imagined? What sounds does your animal make? Where might your animal live?"
Exhibit *12 minutes*	All the students sketch their creatures and describe the color and name. Those who can write put descriptions on their page, and others dictate their descriptions to the book-maker. They all describe their animal orally when presenting the final version to the bookmaker. Read the new version of *Brown Bear, Brown Bear, What Do You See?* with new colors and animals. For each "What do you see?" the children show their drawing of the creature "looking at me."
Reflections *10 minutes*	How did you decide on which animal to draw and what color it should be? Think about extending your creature's behavior in various ways. For instance, after seeing "an aqua elephant looking at me," grey goose might waddle off to a pond or follow other geese down to a garden.

RESOURCE 2

Level: Primary Grades
Subject: Physical Education
Title: Imitating Animals

Situation *50 minutes*	The purpose of this sequence of *situations* is for young students to make further meaning of the rhythmic, patterned story *Brown Bear, Brown Bear, What Do You See?* "Brown bear, brown bear, what do you see? I see a yellow duck looking at me." They engage in rich literature activities by listening to the story or song, drawing new animals, writing a parallel phrase, acting out new behaviors, describing these new behaviors in words, and retelling the story through new pictures and words. After drawing new animals in the previouslearning episode, students then think about how their animal moved, where it went, and what it ate after it saw the next animal. For example, the red goat might bounce to the garden and eat flowers after seeing "a pink salmon looking at me," and the grey goose might waddle off to a pond and eat slugs after seeing "an aqua elephant looking at me." In the order of the new book, individuals act out what their animal did after it saw another animal looking at it and then the whole class imitates each action.
Groupings *1 minute*	A. Students work in the same small groups as in the Drawing Animals learning design to create actions for their new animals. B. They need space and clothes for free movement.
Bridge *5 minutes*	The teacher and students read the new version of *Brown Bear, Brown Bear, What Do You See?* using the new animals and colors on the pages of the new book that they created together.
Questions *10 minutes*	The students think about their animal and decide where it went and what it ate. They each create movements for these actions. Student: "How does my animal move around? Where would it go? What does it eat?" Teacher: "Where does your animal live? What kind of legs does it have? Where might your animal go? What do you think it eats? How many of these animals have four legs? How many of these animals live on land? How many animals were in the new book?"
Exhibit *24 minutes*	In the order of the new book, first the individuals and then the whole class acts out the movements of each animal after it sees another animal looking at it.
Reflections *10 minutes*	Do the actions you created for your animals fit with their habitat? For example, would an orange cow fly or a silver turtle run? Why do you think so? How did you feel imitating your animal?

RESOURCE 3

Level: Primary Grades
Subject: Reading
Title: Retelling the Story

Situation *50 minutes*	The purpose of this sequence of three *situations* is for young students to make further meaning of the rhythmic, patterned story *Brown Bear, Brown Bear, What Do You See?* "Brown bear, brown bear, what do you see? I see a yellow duck looking at me." They engage in rich literature activities by listening to the story or song, drawing new animals, writing a parallel phrase, acting out new behaviors, describing these new behaviors in words, and retelling the story through new pictures and words. Students get a new sheet of paper, draw a picture, and write down how their animal moved, where it went, and what it ate after seeing another animal. The words should describe the story they made up when imitating their animal's actions in the previous learning episode.
Groupings *3 minutes*	A. Students work in small groups of two or three formed by the teacher so there is one writer in each group. B. Materials include pencils, markers, crayons, pieces of paper to fit in the book, glue and scissors.
Bridge *12 minutes*	The teacher shows the pages of the new book. Children try to remember where their animal went and what it ate after seeing another animal. Teacher and children brainstorm and chart words that tell how each animal moved, where it went, and what it ate.
Questions *20 minutes*	Students each draw a new picture showing where their animal went and what it ate after seeing another animal "looking at me." The writers in each group write the descriptions on the new pictures. Student: "How can I write down the words to tell how my animal moved, were it went, or what it ate?" Teacher: "What words describe how your animal moved, where it went, and what it ate? Can you try to write them on a piece of scrap paper?"
Exhibit *10 minutes*	In the order of the new book, students bring up their new drawings and read their new page to the class. The teacher puts each new page into the book so it follows the student's first drawing of a new animal.
Reflections *5 minutes*	How does it feel to write a new book together? How did you choose the words to tell about your animal? How would you change the color or movement of your animal if we did this again?

RESOURCE 4

Level: Intermediate Grades
Subject: Science
Title: Moon View

Situation *90 minutes*	The purpose of this *situation* is to provide investigation of a basic science concept rarely understood by adults and often explained with misconceptions relating to shadows of the earth on the moon. Students work in groups to determine the relationship between the sun, the earth, and the phases of the moon. Each group is asked to explain their thinking through a diagram.
Groupings *5 minutes*	A. Students are put into groups of four based on their zodiac signs. B. Groups work with drawings, pictures, or other objects they spontaneously use to construct models of the relationship.
Bridge *30 minutes*	Students are asked to explain why we have seasons. This is based on a similar question posed to students and faculty at a Harvard graduation ceremony in a film called *A Private Universe* where one out of twenty people gave a correct account while others had misconceptions. After students present their explanations, they watch *A Private Universe*.
Questions *20 minutes*	Groups are asked to draw a diagram of the relationship between the sun, the earth, and the phases of the moon. What are the phases of the moon? Isn't the curve on the moon just the result of the shadow of the earth? Why do we see the moon during the day? Do people on the other side of the earth see the moon in the same phase as we do? Why isn't the moon always in eclipse when the earth is between the moon and the sun? What is an eclipse of the sun? Where is the moon in the sky? How big is the moon compared to the earth? How far is the moon from the earth?
Exhibit *25 minutes*	After each group has an opportunity to work out how to represent the relationship between the sun, the earth, and the moon, the person in each group whose birthday is closest to the day of this learning episode will present the explanation to the class.
Reflections *10 minutes*	The teacher leads a debriefing of the phases and positions of the moon related to the earth and sun. Then students describe individually on index cards why people have misconceptions about phases of the moon.

RESOURCE 5

Level: Intermediate Grades
Subject: Media Technology
Title: Logo

Situation *90 minutes*	The purpose of this *situation* is to make students feel competent to create computer programs not just to consume software others have made. Students are introduced to programming in the Logo language and are challenged to accomplish some basic tasks like measuring the screen vertically, horizontally, and diagonally. Then they review the repeat command and try to write a program for the largest equilateral triangle that they can make on the display screen. Then they review a recursive program and write one for the largest circle they can make on the display screen.
Groupings *10 minutes*	A. Students work in pairs determined by self-report of advanced and basic computer skills. B. Students work in pairs or in small groups on the computer depending upon how many are available.
Bridge *20 minutes*	Students make a list of computer languages that they might know or have heard about. Students are given a list of Logo primitives, shown how to enter them into the program, and asked to explore what each of these functions does to the cursor: FD #, BK #, RT #, LT #, PU, PD, PE, HT, ST, CS, HOME, CLEAN. The teacher leads a brief review of each command and what students thought it meant.
Questions *30 minutes*	*Bridge questions* from students: "Why did my cursor disappear? What is being counted?" Teacher: "What did you type just before your turtle disappeared? What is a pixel? How long is a FD 100 line? The teacher then asks students to accomplish the *situation* tasks. Task *questions* from students: "What does equilateral mean? How many degrees are in a triangle? Why did my triangle look weird?" Teacher: "What two root words are in equilateral and what might they mean? If you took a triangle at one corner and unfolded it flat, what would you have? If you were trying to walk in a triangle, how would you turn corners? Writing the same thing over and over can be tedious, so how might you repeat a routine?"
Exhibit *20 minutes*	When most students are done trying to make the largest equilateral triangle, they show to the class the triangle they made and the program to draw it. Later, students show to the class the circle they made and the program to draw it.
Reflections *10 minutes*	The teacher asks students to compare different programs that draw the same figure. How did it feel when you were in control of what happened on the computer? What image did you have in your mind of the way the cursor was moving based on your commands? Why is Logo called a computer language?

RESOURCE 6

Level: Intermediate Grades
Subject: Special Education
Title: Vending Machines

Situation *90 minutes* *(or more* *depending on* *travel time)*	The purpose of this *situation* is for each student to learn independent life skills and to do some basic problem solving when confronted by a new challenge. Educators support developmentally delayed students as they learn new life skills. These include managing money and using a vending machine. Students are given a $5 bill and asked to use three different vending machines to get a sandwich, a drink, and dessert or chips.
Groupings *10 minutes*	A. The teacher puts students in pairs. When possible, a more capable or street-wise student is teamed with a less able or experienced one. Each student team is also assigned a paraeducator or adult volunteer to accompany them or to shadow them so they are protected or can have assistance as needed B. $5 bill or equivalent change per team is needed.
Bridge *30 minutes* *(or several* *sessions)*	The first part of this *bridge* focuses on breaking down a five-dollar bill into smaller denominations and counting the money. The second part of the *bridge* includes a whole-class visit to a vending machine area so that each child or young person can put coins or paper into a machine, get at least one product out of the machine, and retrieve any change.
Questions *30 minutes* *(or several* *sessions)*	Teachers take students to a vending machine area, give each a $5 bill, and expect them to work in pairs and purchase the items designated in the *situation*. Teacher: "What do you already know about using a vending machine? Where on the machines is information about the product and the cost? What are clues to use if you can't read? What do you do if the machine doesn't take the kind of money you have? What will you do if the machine eats your money but doesn't give you anything?"
Exhibit *10 minutes*	If the team returns to the teacher with any or all of the three parts of the meal, they have a literal exhibit and can describe their experience in words, written or oral. If they don't have items, they can tell what happened.
Reflections *10 minutes*	The teacher invites students to discuss their experiences. Why were you or weren't you successful? What would help you be successful next time? What are some characteristics of vending machines? What are some strategies that will help you use vending machines in the future?

RESOURCE 7

Level: Middle School
Subject: Language Arts
Title: Fairy Tales

Situation *50 minutes*	The purpose of this *situation* is to engage students in analyzing fairy tales so they develop an understanding of core elements and common themes that define this area of literature. Students consider their previous experience with fairy tales, develop their definition of a fairy tale, and identify a list of common elements that are found in fairy tales.
Groupings *5 minutes*	A. Students put themselves into groups of three or four. B. The students are provided with large sheets of chart paper, markers, and tape so they can write their group's definition of a fairy tale and list of common elements in fairy tales and post these for the exhibit. Copies of articles by experts defining fairy tales and listing common characteristics of fairy tales are given to individual students after the exhibit.
Bridge *10 minutes*	The teacher describes personal experiences with fairy tales and asks students to read what they have written the previous day about their personal memories of fairy tales.
Questions *15 minutes*	Students organize into groups and get paper, markers, and tape. They develop their definition of a fairy tale and list common characteristics of fairy tales. What were your previous experiences with fairy tales? How would you define a fairy tale? What are common characteristics of fairy tales? How do your definitions compare with the experts'? Were your definitions and lists as precise? After seeing the other groups' and reading the experts' definitions and lists, what would you add to your own? Which definition was more meaningful to you and would be more helpful in writing your own fairy tale? Why are we studying fairy tales? Where did fairy tales come from? What are fairy tales from other cultures?
Exhibit *10 minutes*	Student groups tape the chart papers with their definition and list of common elements on the white board and present their thinking to the rest of the class.
Reflections *10 minutes*	Students read the articles and discuss the similarities to and contrasts with their own definitions and lists. Then they write about what they would add to their definitions or lists from other groups or from the article. Students describe why their own definition or an expert's definition was more meaningful to them as they think about writing their own fairy tale.

RESOURCE 8

Level: Middle School
Subject: Mathematics
Title: Base Blocks

Situation *One week*	The purpose of this *situation* is to provide a deeper exploration of number sense and place value in a context other than base ten. Students work with models of a base, from base two through base seven, and use them to show how they would solve basic problems requiring addition, subtraction, multiplication, and division. Each group is asked to model the problem, a solution, and the relationship between the two.
Groupings *10 minutes*	A. Students get into six groups by counting off from one to how many there are in the class. Then they divide their number by six and get into groups by remainders; zero, one, two, three, four, and five. B. Groups work with blocks that model a base that is two more than their remainder; remainder zero group works with base two, remainder one with base three, and so on.
Bridge *30 minutes*	Students are each given a sheet with numbers from 0 to 100 on it and asked to work in remainder groups to write each of these numbers in their assigned base. After each group completes the count sheets, they gather all of the pieces that model places in their base from a large pile of base blocks. Students model some of the numbers under 100, and then the teacher reviews the places and exponents for different bases.
Questions *Two or three class periods*	*Bridge questions* from students: "How do we count in our base?" Teacher: "What do we do when we fill up the first place in base ten? What digits do we use in base ten? What digits can you use in your base? What do we do when we fill up the first and second places in base ten?" Give students the following four problems to solve by modeling the problem, a solution, and the relationship between the two: 1. Rosalie goes to the convenience store and buys a can of pop for 43 cents and a candy bar for 34 cents. How much does she spend? 2. Rosalie gives the clerk a dollar bill to pay for her purchase. How much change does she receive? 3. Rosalie goes outside and her brother Jamie asks for her can when she is done. He puts it with eleven other cans that he and his friends have collected, and they will get seven cents per can from the recycler. How much money will they receive? 4. Jamie has to split this money equally with his three friends who helped him collect the cans. How much money will each get from the recycling?
Exhibit *10-15 minutes per question*	After each group has an opportunity to work out how to represent the problem, a solution, and the relationship between the two, the groups have a "see what we made parade," so each group can show its model to others and explain its work.
Reflections *15 minutes*	The teacher discusses the concept of counting in bases with the whole class. Then students write individually on index cards about what they learned and what they were thinking during their work together.

RESOURCE 9

Level: Middle School
Subject: Industrial Technology
Title: Scooter Motor

Situation *One* *quarter*	The purpose of this *situation* is for students to understand how a small gas engine works. This *situation* is structured over one quarter, beginning with teams of students taking apart and reassembling a small gas engine, testing and replacing specific parts of it, testing it on the bench, and then testing it on a machine like a scooter that they make themselves. Throughout the experience, the theory of small engines is reviewed and applied.
Groupings *First class*	A. Teams of 2 to 3 students are determined by the number of students in the class, the number of engines available, and the amount of hands-on learning each student needs. B. For instance, one motor could be taken apart by the teacher and each team given one part. One motor could be taken apart several times, once by each team. Or 4 to 5 motors could be divided among 20 students. The groups should be small enough that each student is fully participating.
Bridge *First week*	Each team of 2 to 3 students is given a part of a small engine. Looking at a schematic, they must identify the part, describe its function, and tell which other parts it interacts with. They might also examine the part to see if it is in good condition or worn and in need of replacement.
Questions *4 to 5* *weeks*	Teams are given a motor to disassemble, reassemble, bench test, mount, and field test by themselves. How does a small gas engine work? Where does the fuel go? What does the spark plug do? What is exhaust composed of? Why does modifying the spark plug or the fuel blend effect the performance? What would happen if the motor were larger or smaller? What else could you do with this motor?
Exhibit *1 to 2 weeks*	The teams can exhibit individual parts of the engine, descriptions of their analysis, and repairs made throughout the term. The final exhibit, of course, is the fully functioning scooter. They should prepare a presentation and demonstration for the whole school.
Reflections *1 week to* *write, edit,* *and put on* *a web page*	The teacher leads ongoing analysis of gas-engine repair based on problems that students encounter. What did you know about small gas engines at the beginning of the term? What was the most difficult concept to understand? How did you make sense of that concept, teach it to others on your team, or demonstrate that you now understood it? If you were to teach a class about small gas engines, how would you proceed? Given the movement away from use of small gas engines toward electric ones, is small gas-engine repair an important skill?

RESOURCE 10

Level: High School
Subject: Social Studies
Title: Trading Partners

Situation *6 weeks*	The purpose of this *situation* is for students to investigate how global trade will influence their future employment. Students explore international trade between continents and determine how it might affect their future jobs. Teachers can specify region, goods or services, and jobs, depending on the required curriculum. The students list jobs of family and friends then review the want ads to see the kinds of positions that employers are seeking to fill. Students choose an occupation and company for the duration of the unit, then list ways it is linked to international trade.
Groupings *First day*	A. Maps of the six inhabited continents are cut into four to six puzzle-like pieces and distributed randomly to students. They organize into six groups by finding others with pieces of the same continent. B. Accompanying materials include maps, graphs, business pages, and website information related to international trade.
Bridge *1 week*	Groups conduct a preliminary study of current trading activities within their continent. For instance, the South America group might choose citrus fruit if the curriculum includes the role of trade agreements and foreign subsidies among different nations. Citrus fruit is also a good choice for Florida or California students.
Questions *2 weeks*	Students select an occupation and evaluate its relationship to international trade. What are the roles and responsibilities of your occupation? What goods or services does your company produce or offer and how are they used in the local region? Nationally? Internationally? Is there a link between what you do and the products of any of the six continents we talked about? How will your occupation be affected by changes in international trade?
Exhibit *2 weeks*	Each continent group prepares a multimedia presentation about the influence that international trading activities will have on their occupations. The class develops a rubric to assess each presentation.
Reflections *1 week*	Reflect on your continent, country, and region in relation to the original question. Given what you have learned about trade between your region and the world, what are the implications for your chosen occupation? Document your reflections as a list of implications, recommendations for job preparation, or plans for a job search. Complete a form including name, date of birth, chosen occupation, international trading factors influencing that occupation, and your personal goals for training in that occupation.

RESOURCE 11

Level: High School
Subject: Foreign Language
Title: Spanish Songs

Situation *2 weeks*	The purpose of this *situation* is to explore the influence of Hispanic language and culture on American music. Students transcribe a contemporary Spanish song by Selena in the tejano style popular with Mexican Americans and some mainstream audiences. They create an English translation of the lyrics to fit the melody and rhythm of the original Spanish version. Finally, students conduct research on the Internet to consider how Hispanic musical styles have influenced mainstream American music.
Groupings *First day*	A. Students are grouped based on the number of letters in their Spanish names. No group should be larger than 4. B. Each group needs a CD or cassette player and a computer with Internet access.
Bridge *First day*	Invite students to discuss what they know about tejano music or Selena. Watch the film *Selena* if they are not familiar with Mexican American tejano music. Students should consider her experience as a Mexican American who learned Spanish as a second language and debate whether she would have been successful singing only Spanish lyrics or only English lyrics.
Questions *5-6 days*	Students transcribe the song *La Carcacha* from Spanish into English and then conduct research on the Internet to consider how Hispanic culture has influenced mainstream American music. Students: "How would we translate this verse?" Teacher: "Can you make your translation fit the melody and rhythm? How have Hispanic musical styles influenced mainstream American music? Is there such a thing as mainstream American music when many styles such as jazz, reggae, or R&B are rooted in other cultures? Would her music be as interesting and successful if the lyrics were always in English? "
Exhibit *2 days*	Groups sing their transcribed song in English. In Spanish, they present their findings about how Hispanic musical styles have influenced mainstream American music.
Reflections *1 day*	The teacher leads a discussion on the challenges of transcribing lyrics into English. Students write journal entries to answer these questions. Why did Selena's music "crossover" into the mainstream music scene in the U.S? How has your music listening influenced your knowledge of subcultures in the U.S.? What is the place of music in crosscultural understanding?

RESOURCE 12

Level: High School
Subject: Business Education
Title: Creating Spreadsheets

Situation *1 week*	The purpose of this *situation* is for students to create spreadsheets with categories, formulas, and charts to make and account for a personal budget. Students create a spreadsheet with categories for all their income and spending for a week. Each day they record in a notebook the money they get and spend and then transfer this information to their spreadsheet during class.
Groupings *First day*	A. Students work in pairs on computers and with each other to develop categories, formulas, and a system to track their income and spending. Then they work in teams of four to record class information. B. Materials include one computer per pair, notebooks, index cards, Monopoly money.
Bridge *First day*	The teacher hands out index cards and asks students to put down anonymously the amount of money they get and spend each week. Then the teacher tallies these results with the class and discusses what categories might be used to present this information. For instance, under $20, $20 to $39, $40 to $59, $60 to $79, $80 to $99, and $100 or over. Then the teacher creates a spreadsheet with the tallied information and draws a chart showing the distribution. Teacher and students brainstorm the possible categories of income and spending: food, clothing, entertainment, transportation, games, computers, books, or sports.
Questions *3 days*	Students create and update their spreadsheets for a personal budget. Student: "If I don't have a job, what should I do?" Teacher: "Do you have an allowance or get money from your parents for lunch or the bus? What categories will you develop to describe your spending?"
Exhibit *Last day*	On Friday, students create and print a graph of their spreadsheet and then print six copies of their anonymous spreadsheet for classmates. They work in teams of four to consolidate the separate spreadsheets into a common class spreadsheet and present their results to the class.
Reflections *Last day*	The teacher leads the class in considering the similarities and differences in group spreadsheets. In what categories did you expect to find the most income or spending? What surprised you most about the class's expenses or income? How would you use a spreadsheet to balance a checkbook?

References

Allen, Dwight W. (1969). *Microteaching [by] Dwight Allen [and] Kevin Ryan.* Reading, MA: Addison-Wesley.

Aronson, Elliot. (1978). *The jigsaw classroom.* Beverly Hills, CA: Sage.

Ausubel, David Paul. (1968). *Educational psychology: A cognitive view.* New York: Holt, Rinehart & Winston.

Block, James. (1971). *Mastery learning: Theory and practice.* New York: Holt, Rinehart & Winston.

Bloom, Benjamin et al. (Eds.). (1956/1964). *Taxonomy of educational objectives: The classification of educational goals, by a committee of college and university examiners.* New York: Longmans, Green.

Boyer, Ernest. (1995). *The basic school.* Princeton, NJ: Carnegie Foundation for the Advancement of Teaching.

Brody, Celeste, & Davidson, Neil. (1998). *Professional development for cooperative learning: Issues and approaches.* New York: State University of New York Press.

Brookfield, Stephen. (1995). *Becoming a critically reflective teacher.* San Francisco: Jossey-Bass.

Brooks, Jacqueline G., & Brooks, Martin G. (1993). *The case for constructivist classrooms.* Alexandria, VA: Association for Supervision and Curriculum Development.

Brosterman, Norman. (1997). *Inventing kindergarten: Nineteenth-century children, twentieth-century art.* New York: Harry N. Abrams.

Bruner, Jerome S. (1996). *The culture of education.* Cambridge, MA: Harvard University Press.

Carini, Patricia F. (1986). Building from children's strengths. *Journal of Education, 168*(3), 13-24.

Case, Robbie. (1996). Changing views of knowledge and their impact on educational research and practice. In D. R. Olson & N. Torrance (Eds.), *The handbook of education and human development* (pp. 75-99). Cambridge, MA: Blackwell.

Clandinin, D. Jean., & Connelly, F. Michael. (1994). Personal experience methods. In N. K. Denzin & Y. S. Lincoln (Eds.), *Handbook of qualitative research*. Thousand Oaks, CA: Sage.

Cohen, Elizabeth. (1994). *Designing groupwork: Strategies for the heterogeneous classroom* (2nd ed.). New York: Teachers College Press.

Collay, Michelle. (1998). Recherche: Teaching our life histories. *Teaching and Teacher Education, 14*(3), 245-255.

Collay, Michelle, Dunlap, Diane, Enloe, Walter, & Gagnon, George. (1998). *Learning circles: Creating conditions for professional development*. Thousand Oaks, CA: Corwin.

Collier, Virginia P. (1995). *Promoting academic success for ESL students: Understanding second language acquisition for school*. Elizabeth: New Jersey Teaching English to Speakers of Other Languages-Bilingual Education.

Cuban, Larry. (1984). *How teachers taught: Constancy and change in American classrooms, 1890-1980*. New York: Longman.

Dewey, John. (1964). Why reflective thinking must be an educational aim. *John Dewey on Education*. Chicago: University of Chicago Press. (Original work published 1933)

Dewey, John. (1974). My pedagogic creed. In R. D. Archbambaum (Ed.), *John Dewey on education*. Chicago: University of Chicago Press. (Original work published 1897)

Dienes, Zoltan Paul. (1967). *Building up mathematics*. London: Hutchinson Educational.

Dietz, Mary. (1995). Using portfolios as a framework for professional development. *Journal of Staff Development, 16*(2), 40-43.

Duckworth, Eleanor. (1987). *The having of wonderful ideas*. New York: Teachers College Press.

Duncan, Isadora. (1926). *The art of the dance*. New York: Theatre Arts Books.

Engel, Brenda. (1994). Portfolio assessment and the new paradigm: New instruments and new places. *Educational Forum, 59*(1), 22-27.

Flanders, Ned. (1970). *Analyzing teaching behavior.* Reading, MA: Addison-Wesley.

Fosnot, Catherine. (1996). *Constructivism: Perspectives, theory, and practice.* New York: Teachers College Press.

Freire, Paulo. (1970). *Pedagogy of the oppressed.* New York: Seabury.

Furth, H. (1966). *Thinking without language: Psychological implications of deafness.* New York: Free Press.

Gagne, Robert M. (1985). *The conditions of learning and theory of instruction.* (4th ed.). New York: Holt, Rinehart & Winston.

Gagnon, George, & Collay, Michelle. (1996). *Teachers' perspectives on constructivist learning design.* Presented at Second Annual Qualitative Research Conference, St. Paul, MN.

Gallagher, James J., Nuthall, G. A., & Rosenshine, B. (1970). *Classroom observation.* Chicago: Rand McNally.

Geist, Pamela K., & Remillard, Janine T. (1998, April). *What an innovative curriculum for teachers reveals about teachers' professional learning.* Paper presented at American Educational Research Association, San Diego, CA.

Goodlad, John. (1984). *A place called school: Prospects for the future.* New York: McGraw-Hill.

Greene, Maxine. (1995). *Releasing the imagination: Essays on education, the arts, and social change.* San Francisco: Jossey-Bass.

Harvard-Smithsonian Center for Astrophysics Science Education Department, Science Media Group. (1987). *A private universe.* Burlington, VT: Annenburg/CPB Math & Science Collection. Available on the World Wide Web: http://www.learner.org/catalog/science/pup/

Hirsch, E. D. (1987). *Cultural literacy: What every American needs to know.* Boston: Houghton Mifflin.

Hunter, Madeleine. (1982). *Mastery teaching.* El Segundo, CA: TIP.

Johnson, David, & Johnson, Roger. (1998). *Learning together and alone: Cooperative, competitive, and individualistic learning.* Boston: Allyn & Bacon.

Kagan, Spencer. (1990). *Cooperative learning: Resources for teachers.* San Juan Capistrano, CA: Resources for Teachers.

Krashen, Stephen. (1997, March-April). Bilingualism and bilingual education: Good for English, good for the bilingual, good for society. *American Language Review,* 12-32.

Kuhn, Thomas. (1996.). *The structure of scientific revolutions.* Chicago: University of Chicago Press.

Lambert, Linda. (1998). *Building leadership capacity in schools.* Alexandria, VA: Association for Supervision and Curriculum Development.

Lambert, Linda, Collay, Michelle, Dietz, Marey E., Kent, Karen, & Richert, Anna E. (1997). *Who will save our schools? Teachers as constructivist leaders.* Thousand Oaks, CA: Corwin.

Meier, Deborah. (1995). *The power of their ideas: Lessons for America from a small school in Harlem.* Boston: Beacon.

Mezirow, Jack. (1990). *Fostering critical reflection in adulthood: A guide to transformative and emanicipatory learning.* San Francisco: Jossey-Bass.

Montessori, Maria. (1963). *Education for a new world.* Aydar, Madras, India: Kalakshetra.

Montessori, Maria. (1965). *Dr. Montessori's own handbook.* New York: Schocken Books.

National Center for Education Statistics. (1998). *Pursuing excellence: Initial findings from the Third International Math and Science Study* [Video samples from the video tape from Third International Math and Science Study video tape classroom study in Germany, Japan and the United States] [CD-ROM]. Washington, DC: Government Printing Office.

Papert, Seymour. (1993). *The children's machine: Rethinking school in the age of the computer.* New York: Basic Books.

Perrone, Vito. (Ed.). (1991a). *Expanding student assessment.* Alexandria, VA: Association for Supervision and Curriculum Development.

Perrone, Vito. (1991b). *A letter to teachers: Reflections on schooling and the art of teaching.* San Francisco: Jossey-Bass.

Piaget, Jean. (1976). *To understand is to invent: The future of education* (G-A. Roberts, Trans.). New York: Penguin.

Piaget, Jean, & Inhelder, Barbel. (1969). *The psychology of the child.* New York: Basic Books.

Sadker, Myra, & Sadker, David. (1994). *Failing at fairness: How American schools cheat girls.* New York: Simon & Schuster.

Sanders, Norris. (1966). *Classroom questions: What kinds?* New York: Harper & Row.

Sapon-Shevin, Mara. (1999). *Because we can change the world: A practical guide to building cooperative, inclusive, classroom communities.* Boston: Allyn & Bacon.

Schmuck, Richard A. (1997). *Practical action research for change.* Arlington Heights, IL: Skylight.

Schmuck, Richard, & Schmuck, Patricia. (1997). *Group processes in the classroom.* Madison, WI: Brown & Benchmark.

Schøn, Donald. (1983). *The reflective practitioner: How professionals think in action.* New York: Basic Books.

Sharan, Shlomo, & Sharan, Yael. (1976). *Small group teaching.* Englewood Cliffs, NJ: Educational Technology.

Sharan, Shlomo, & Sharan, Yael. (1992). *Expanding cooperative learning through group investigation.* New York: Teachers College Press.

Shulman, Lee. (1999). Taking learning seriously. Change, (New Rochelle), 31(4), 11-17.

Sizer, Theodore. (1992). *Horace's school: Redesigning the American high school.* Boston: Houghton Mifflin.

Slavin, Robert E. (1983). *Cooperative learning.* New York: Longman.

Slavin, Robert E. (1987). *Cooperative learning: Student teams.* Washington, DC: National Endowment for the Arts.

Steffe, Leslie P., & D'Ambrosio, Beatriz S. (1995). Toward a working model of constructivist teaching: A reaction to Simon. *Journal for Research in Mathematics Education, 26*(2), 146-159.

Stigler, James W., & Hiebert, James. (1999). *The teaching gap: Best ideas from the world's teachers for improving education in the classroom.* New York: Free Press.

Taba, Hilda, Durkin, Mary C., Fraenkel, Jack R., & McNaughton, Anthony H. (1971). *A teacher's handbook to elementary social studies: An inductive approach* (2nd ed.). Reading, MA: Addison-Wesley.

Tyler, Ralph. (1949). *Basic principles of curriculum and instruction.* Chicago: University of Chicago Press.

Vygotsky, Lev S. (1986). *Thought and language* (A. Kozulin, Ed. & Trans.). Cambridge: MIT Press.

WGBH Boston. (1997). *Teaching math: A video library.* Burlington, VT: Annenburg/CPB Math and Science Collection. Available on the World Wide Web: http://www.learner.org/catalog/math

Wiggins, Grant. (1998). *Educative assessment: Designing assessments to inform and improve student performance.* San Francisco, CA: Jossey-Bass.

Witherell, Carol, & Noddings, Nel. (Eds.). (1991). *Stories lives tell: Narrative and dialogue in education.* New York: Teachers College Press.

Index

160

CORWIN
PRESS

The Corwin Press logo—a raven striding across an open book—represents the happy union of courage and learning. We are a professional-level publisher of books and journals for K–12 educators, and we are committed to creating and providing resources that embody these qualities. Corwin's motto is "Success for All Learners."